THE BIG BOOK OF

MAJOR
MUM
HACKS

THE BIG BOOK OF
MAJOR MUM HACKS

CASEY MAJOR-BUNCE

SPHERE

SPHERE

First published in Great Britain in 2025 by Sphere

1 2 3 4 5 6 7 8 9 10

A CIP catalogue record for this book
is available from the British Library.

ISBN 978-1-4087-3376-9

Photographer: Nicky Johnston
Photographer's Assistant: Max Spanner
Copy Editor: Abi Smith
Design and illustrations D.R. ink
Printed and bound in China by C&C Offset Printing Co., Ltd.

Papers used by Sphere are from well-managed forests
and other responsible sources.

Sphere
An imprint of
Little, Brown Book Group
Carmelite House
50 Victoria Embankment
London EC4Y 0DZ

An Hachette UK Company
www.hachette.co.uk

www.littlebrown.co.uk

Contents

HOME

ON THE GO 🔔

SUMMER ☀

AUTUMN 🍁 WINTER ❄️

SPECIAL OCCASIONS

Introduction

Hello my lovelies and welcome to my very first book of Major Mum Hacks that is accessible to everyone – and I mean the whole family, because no matter who you are, where you come from, how you learn, this book is for you.

I want anyone who picks up this book to feel empowered, because ultimately what I'm sharing here are ways that I know have helped me, personally, to navigate motherhood; hacks that have saved me effort and money, saved my sanity and, most importantly, my time.

Time is so special when you are a mum. It's something you can't buy and it's something there never seems to be enough of. But I am hoping that, with this book, I can help you use your time wisely and therefore enjoy the important things in life more regularly. Making memories with your children is so important, and we put such an emphasis on being the perfect mum or feeling like we are failing if we can't do it all.

" Ways to enjoy more time with our children. Ways to navigate the stresses and pressure that we unnecessarily put on ourselves to be perfect."

The most beautiful people I know are those who have known suffering, known frustrations and found themselves struggling to find a way to cope with all that life demands of them. These people have an appreciation, a sensitivity and an understanding that fills them with compassion. People just like my own mum, Becky.

Mum taught me a lesson when I was very young, about creating a magical childhood, even if the odds are against you. When I was six years old, she gave birth to my younger brother. But then she became very ill. She became disabled through her illness, and the trouble was her illness was so unique the doctors didn't know what was causing it and whether it might be contagious, so they kept her away from us.

For around nine months we weren't allowed to see our mum, and our family dynamic changed very quickly. Dad was left to care for three children: me, my elder brother, who was twelve, and my younger brother, who was just a few months old.

When Mum finally came home, she was different. She had gone from being an active woman who took us swimming and went on family walks in the countryside, to a mum who would feel tired after half an hour and would spend her days in a wheelchair. And that meant we spent most of our days at home because my dad couldn't push my mum around in a wheelchair and push a baby at the same time – not to mention having to control two other children. But Mum never gave up on being a mum. She couldn't take us for long walks any more but she could still create memories for us, be the best she could be, but in ways that she adapted and made work for us and for her.

"I see the world a little bit differently and I love being able to help others when they come to me with, 'Case, I need your help! How can I make this?'"

© Casey Major-Bunce

(L-R) My brother Jamie, cousin Liz, me, my cousin Kyle and brother Clancy. Some of the best times of my childhood were the simplest, least fancy and least expensive.

So instead of making cupcakes with us, which would involve lots of equipment and ingredients and tidying up afterwards, she would buy fairy cakes from the shop, remove the cheap icing and then we'd spend time having fun with her decorating the cakes with our own toppings.

She knew she had to manage her time more efficiently because of how tired she would get, and we enjoyed doing fun things with her – because who doesn't like spending time with their mum as a kid? My mum knew that, and she adjusted to her life being different – she had to find 'cheat' ways to help create those memories.

Some of the best days I ever had were the simplest, least fancy and least expensive. Like having sleepovers with my brothers and my cousins, Liz and Kyle, looking up at the stars, toasting marshmallows, thinking it was so exciting to be awake at 9 pm! Or going to the park with them, making dens in our house, or being with family for dinner – being surrounded by love was just everything.

So, this is really where my hacks probably began – in the midst of my own childhood. And I love bringing that idea back, like recipes passing on to the next generation, ways to make our lives easier. Ways to enjoy more time with our children. Ways to navigate the stresses and pressure that we unnecessarily put on ourselves to be perfect. Why do we do that? Honestly, why? And then if we have a 'bad' day, we think we are failures. What's that all about? Who dictates what makes us a failure?

I will say this until I'm blue in the face, but here it is: one bad day does not make you a bad mum. Ditto for one bad week or one bad month. It does not make you A. Bad. Mum. Stop beating yourself up. And – *spoiler alert* – nobody who ever thought they were a bad mum actually is.

We feel like we are failing if we can't do it all, and we feel like we are cheating

> **If anyone thinks I am some super-sussed, ducks-in-a-row mum, please know that I am the biggest worrier ... I have pigeons all over the place."**

if we cut corners – but cutting corners or using hacks or being clever with our time simply means we don't lose out on any of the joy. And life is too short to miss out on any of that joy.

There are moments in our lives that shape us for ever. Sometimes we can't let go of certain memories because they are constant reminders of a great story that we never expected to end. Watching my twins play and grow up together reminds me of my cousin and me – we were so close and we did everything together growing up.

When she died of meningitis, my world ended. We had just started the second year of secondary school and from that point on, everything changed. So believe me when I say I know about time, I know that you have to appreciate what you have at the time and in some ways, giving my children the best memories is everything to me. It's a way of healing what I lost and I think we can all relate to loss and healing ourselves through our children because every moment is a gift.

Which is why I am so proud to bring you this book which celebrates making the most of everything, no matter your situation.

I have always been that sort of mum that's been asked by other mums about fixing this or making that because I am a problem solver. I am autistic and dyslexic, and I have always had to find ways of being able to adapt to situations, to find my own way because conventional ways were tricky and tiring and over-stimulating.

I see the world a little bit differently and I love being able to help others when they come to me with, 'Case, I need your help! How can I make this?'

My hacks spiralled from there. One of my friends said I should put some of them on Instagram and my first thought was, 'Don't be daft, who's going to want to see that!'

If anyone thinks I am some super-sussed, ducks-in-a-row mum, please know that I am the biggest worrier, I have no confidence in myself and I have pigeons all over the place. I am confident that everyone else knows what they are doing, but I will criticise and question and judge myself until the cows come home. I am without a doubt my own worst critic, so my wonderful husband, Zues (spelled like that because I am dyslexic, remember, although that's not his real name, just a pet name I gave him that's stuck!), and my family know they never need to say anything – I'll be beating myself up already.

But I am also the biggest believer that things are meant to be. When I posted my first hack – one about Halloween – in October 2022, I was nervous but at the same time thought I had nothing to lose. Because things do work out in the end, whatever life throws at you. And there is no such thing as having your life sorted or being perfect.

Growing up, I think I realised that sooner than most people. I went to an all-girls school – I had to get the bus and I would always lose my bus ticket. Always. My parents had to give me extra bus money each day because they knew I'd lose it. Then, one day, I came home and I had lost a shoe! My mum was like, 'How?!' And I didn't know the answer. I think then I was showing some of the early signs of autism and I remember I did find the transition to secondary school really hard, so much so that I had counselling. But back then no one really understood why I was struggling and what was going on.

So believe me (again!) when I say I get the idea that people find things tricky, that we are all trying our best and that we all want ways to make our lives easier.

And I hope you find some of my hacks useful. They are problem-solvers. They are things you didn't know you needed but that might well have a big impact.

I know full well that if my cousin were here with me right now she would be my biggest cheerleader. Which is why it's important for us to stick together, right? To help each other, and to share the ideas and the tricks and the tools that have shaped us, to help us navigate this thing called Motherhood in the best way possible.

Some memories never leave you, they're in your bones, and wouldn't it be wonderful if we could create such magical times for our children without feeling like we are failing if we don't get everything right?

I'm Major Mum Hacks and I'm so pleased you're here.

Much love,

Casey x
aka Major Mum Hacks

Essentials list

There are lots of items I would call 'essentials' that I use for many of my hacks in this book, so if you like to be prepared (and who doesn't?) here's a list of the basics that feature most often. Think of it as creating your very own store cupboard of hack ingredients.

★ Effervescent tablets

★ Art caddy

★ Balloons

★ Cable ties

★ Disposable gloves

★ Double-sided tape

★ Edible eyes

★ Edible glue

★ Empty plastic bottles (it's great to keep a supply of these)

★ Glow sticks

★ Glue gun

★ Kids' stickers (although you probably have a million of these around the house)

★ Masking tape

★ Muffin tin

★ PVA glue

★ Shoe organiser

★ Silicone cupcake holders

★ Velcro dots

★ Zipped sandwich bags

Mums are everything, all at once: chefs, personal assistants, teachers, chauffeurs, event planners, birthday party organisers, nurses, dentists, and defenders against bad dreams.

Which is why our homes are the place we need to be the most efficient so we can spend more time making memories with the people that mean the most to us.

These are some of my favourite hacks for making everyday home life both simple and satisfying. I've broken them up into sections so you can navigate easily to hacks that will help you in any given situation.

The Home

1. Puzzle hack

If you ever have a spare five minutes and enjoy doing a puzzle, you'll know how blinking annoying it is when you come to the end only to find a piece missing.*

So imagine that frustration, multiplied by about a million and one if you are a toddler and you want to do your favourite puzzle for the umpteenth time and you can't find the last wooden piece.**

Banish the upset for them by using a few self-adhesive Velcro dots instead.

★ Simply take each puzzle piece and add one half of a Velcro dot to the underside

★ Take the other half of each Velcro dot and add it to the corresponding part of the puzzle board

★ The pieces will then stay attached when they are matched up and won't fall out

★ Not only is the puzzle now easier to store, but also you'll never have any tears over missing pieces again!***

* Swear words are uttered
** A tantrum will ensue
*** From either you or your toddler

2. Sandwich bag and board games hack

HACK THE HACK:
Why not keep your dice in a little see-through plastic container/tub but also use them in that container while you are playing? You won't have runaway dice ever again!

This is a winner if your family like playing games but you end up spending too much time hunting around for dice or half the playing cards you know you have somewhere at the back of the cupboard.

It's also great if you have a mountain of board game boxes that take up too much space, look untidy and invariably get knocked over so that the pieces escape from lids that have come loose.

Sandwich bags, especially ziplock ones, are therefore your BGBF (board game best friend) and ideal for keeping everything stored together and more accessible.

★ Empty your board game's contents into a bag and either cut out the name label/photo from the box or write the game's name on a separate piece of paper and put it inside the bag

★ Now all the bits you need for each game are in a see-through, clearly marked bag that can be ziplocked shut

★ Not only do the bags take up less storage space, they are also easier to find and you can keep any flat boards that are needed for the game in a neat, far less bulky pile. Winner!

3. Shoe divider for dolls, action figures and building blocks hack

Playing with dolls is a never-ending game in our house but quite often they'll be scattered around, left upstairs/downstairs/on the stairs and there is never anywhere to put them after little imaginations have gone to sleep.

Instead of storing them on top of each other in a messy pile, dolls and action figures can have their own personal space with this handy shoe-hanger hack. It's also a great storage solution for building blocks and keeping all the bricks colour-coded together.

★ Hang a see-through shoe divider on the back of your child's door or in their wardrobe and give each doll their own standing section

★ For building block fans, you can use the dividers to sort all the building blocks into colours, which is not only hugely satisfying but also a great way for your child to clearly see what they have

★ There's a variety of different sized shoe dividers online, so you can adapt to your space and the amount of dolls/volume of building blocks you have

★ And did I mention it's hugely satisfying?

HACK THE HACK:
Obviously as your children get older and become trainer-hoarders, the shoe storage racks will remain a valuable purchase.

4. Tape on pen lid hack

No longer will you sound like a broken record – 'Don't forget to put the lid back on!' – when your coloured felt-tip pens are being used, because this hack will take away the need for any such utterance to pass your lips. You're welcome.

It's also a good way to keep all your pens together too, so you won't have a missing marker at a crucial colouring-in moment – this is a real and stressful phenomenon.

★ Get some tape – masking tape works well, but if you have stronger packing tape or heavy-duty tape that will be fine too – and lay out all the pens you want to tape together on a flat surface

★ Tape across the surface of the lids with the pens lined up, and make sure you take the tape around the back of the lids too

★ You should now have an assembly line of pens with the lids stuck next to each other, allowing pens to be pulled out and put back together after use

★ Not only will you be able to keep tabs on which pens are missing, you can keep them all stored together

★ You can adapt this hack if you like to keep your pens in a pencil case, by taping just three or four together at a time

★ Or you could use a glue gun and glue the lids top down onto a plastic make-up divider. This is good for pens that you want to keep on a desk or somewhere specific

5. Wardrobe toy storage hack

Cuddly, snuggly, loveable and packed with memories, soft toys are the staple of any child's bed. Until they can't actually sleep in their bed, because the teddies have taken over.

Now that Toy Story has forever changed the way we look at toys, which means giving those fluffy animals an annual audit is out of the question, this space-saving hack will help you keep all of your child's much loved cuddlies organised.

★ Using a wardrobe organiser cube, simply pop all the toys into individual sections

★ Each cube (normally a cube will have about five different segments) should be deep enough to fill with several teddies and you can separate them however you prefer – into animals, colours, sizes, etc.

★ These organisers fit nicely into a wardrobe if you are tight on space, or can be hung by a hook on the bedroom wall for easy access

★ Picking a well-loved bedtime companion has never been so easy

6. Magnetic tape toy car hack

Finding a practical way to store toy cars that doesn't involve your carpet looking like a car park can be tricky. But I love that this hack is both sensible and fun for your littler racers – and keeps your floor space clear too. You'll be doing a victory lap in celebration before you know it!

★ Cut some self-adhesive magnetic tape to roughly the length of the car you are going to attach it to

★ Stick the magnetic tape onto the side of your child's chest of drawers, making sure there is space in between strips

★ Add as many rows as you need, then start collecting up the metal cars and hang them on the tape

★ Have fun sorting the cars and attaching them to the strips, creating your own starting grid for a Formula One race to the Moon

★ If you have lots of cars you could use this hack on the side of a wardrobe for more space, or the side of a bedside table to keep all their special motors close

7. Beanbag teddy hack

Beanbags are a great place to flop and chill, and my children love lolloping all over them when reading a book. But instead of spending money on buying a filling for the bag, simply fill it with their teddies and cuddly toys.

★ Gather up cuddly toys and anything soft

★ Fill the bag with as many soft toys as required, depending on your bag size or how squidgy you like the beanbag to be

★ And – hey presto! – an extra-comfy seating, lying, chilling area. Perfect if you're hosting play dates or sleepovers and you might have extra children needing space to flop

★ It's a good way to keep all the extra teddies and soft toys that would otherwise be lying around tidied away and contained

HACK THE HACK:
If you haven't got a beanbag covering why not use an old duvet cover and fill that halfway? You can either just fold over the excess material to make it smaller or cut off the material and sew on your own Velcro strips to make a sealable opening.

8. Apple cutter for potatoes and onions hack

Apple cutters are great for getting equal and perfectly shaped portions of fruit for snack time, but they can also create the perfect potato wedge or help you slice an onion without the need for any sharp knives.

★ Wash each potato and place on a chopping board

★ Push the apple cutter down firmly on each potato and see the wedges spring out. You'll get restaurant-worthy results every time!

★ If your children prefer the straight-cut variety, use the middle section of the potato too

★ For the onions, first cut the ends off and remove the peel. Then push the apple cutter down on each onion, but not all the way, and you'll get small pieces of onion without the need for a knife. And you'll have chopped it so fast you won't have time for your eyes to water. Boom!

★ You can use the apple cutter on fruits too, such as peeled kiwi fruit or peeled pineapple

★ If you want super-fine segments for a fruit salad, first slice the peeled fruits then place the slices into piles of two or three before using the cutter

MAJOR MUM
HACKS VIDEO

9. Strawberry and cherry straw hack

For how many years have we chewed through a cherry before spitting out the pip? Well, no more! And do you want a quick and easy way to get the green bits off the top of strawberries using a straw?

Prepare your bowl of fruit the easy way with this straw-berry hack (like what I did there?!), which is easy enough for little hands to help you with too.

★ For strawberries, fluff up the green leaves and position the straw at the other end of the fruit, then push it up all the way through until the straw comes out of the top with the leaves

★ If you've already given them a quick rinse they are good to go, otherwise run the strawberries under the tap and then start piling up your bowl of juicy goodness

★ Pitting cherries with a straw is just as simple: simply push the straw all the way through the cherry and the pip will come out the other side

MAJOR MUM
HACKS VIDEO

10. Cling film banana hack

We love bananas in our house, but if we're not careful we get to the end of the week and the lovely yellow fruits have gone spotty and brown, and no one wants to eat them.

I hate waste so this hack is a real lifesaver for me and saves me going bananas at the thought of throwing away good fruit.

★ As soon as you have bought your bunch of bananas, grab a piece of cling film and wrap it around the top of every banana in the bunch

★ Then take some more cling film and wrap it around the whole top section/ stem of the bunch and secure it in place if you need to with some tape/ elastic bands

★ There is some clever science afoot, which means that the cling film stops a gas being released and preserves the life of the bananas for longer than normal, meaning that they won't go brown and squidgy as quickly as they otherwise would

★ And that means you have nice yellow 'nanas to eat and not throw away

11. Pizza and pancake cutting hack

Similar to the apple cutter that doesn't just work on apples, just because you are told something works for a specific purpose, that doesn't mean it's the only thing it's good for. Sometimes – whisper it – it's good to break the rules.

★ For example, I like to keep a spare pair of kitchen scissors in my drawer to cut up pizza quickly and easily

★ The scissors will not only cut through the pizza into perfect slices but will go through tougher crusts too

★ Don't ditch your pizza cutter, though – use that to cut your fluffy pancakes into small pieces

★ Basically, this hack is about thinking of ways to adapt your utensils to make your life easier. I found I was endlessly rolling my pizza cutter up and down over the same bit of pizza before I would get a piece, now I simply snip and have a slice!

12. Utensils and pans organisation hack

Everyone has one of those kitchen drawers or cupboards that contains countless cookie cutters, baking trays, (the dreaded) plastic lids and no container … the list could go on. And you can never find anything when you want it, obviously. So why not turn your otherwise frantic-hair-pulling-out cupboard into an organised dream, with the help of some good old-fashioned filing folders?

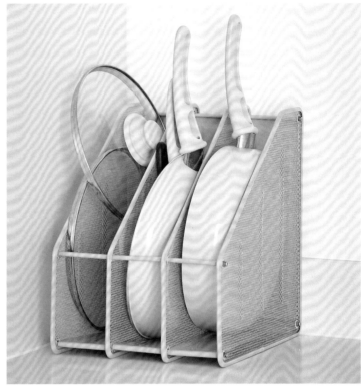

★ Don't worry if you don't have one of these fabulous stationery items already at home. There are plenty of options to buy, with many variations and colours available to suit your space and style

★ I like the metal ones as they are slightly more robust than cardboard ones, and I can wipe them down and clean them more easily if I need to

★ You can line them up in rows and behind each other as they are slim enough to fit several to a cupboard. Instantly that cupboard of tricky-to-store kitchen items becomes a place of calm

★ Labelling your boxes as well means that if you ask your children to get out what they need they can clearly see what they are looking for and everything then gets put back in the right spot too

13. Picture frame shopping list hack

I used to write shopping list notes on scraps of paper and then lose them or throw them away accidentally. With this hack, though, not only do I have a pretty focal point but a rather useful place to make my shopping list.

★ Take a nice picture frame that you no longer use – or have a hunt in a second-hand shop for one

★ I have an A4 sized frame as I need space for long lists, but you can go bigger or smaller depending on your food shopping requirements!

★ Take some pretty coloured paper, nice wrapping paper or even some fabric if you have some spare, and put it in the frame

★ Give the glass a good clean and then dry it

★ Hang the frame in a useful spot so that everyone can use it

★ Take a white chalk marker pen and add things to your list as you go – most photo frames have a nice thickish edge so you can rest the pen on it, or secure with some string and masking tape if needed. Then when you do your online shop you're all set!

★ Chalk markers rub off with a little glass cleaner, so you can start afresh the following week. Or if you are heading out to the shop, don't forget to take a quick photo before you go.

HACK THE HACK:
Shopping lists are just one option for these frames. You can keep them as general household memo boards or give them as cute little gifts to friends, with a nice little message or quote.

14. Cereal cup hack

If you have young children who love to eat cereal in the morning but tend to spill the contents of their bowl everywhere, why not be creative with your crockery and give them a mug to use instead?

★ While you are making your cuppa in the morning, take out an extra mug from the cupboard and fill it half full with their favourite cereal

★ You can then top it up with milk and pass the cup to your child, who can hold on tight to the handle

★ They will be more in control of the mug and less likely to spill any milk over themselves (or anywhere else)

★ And, after they have finished eating, they will find it easier to drink any milk that's left over

★ If you have fussy eaters or kids who can't decide between their cereals, you could fill up two smaller cups to keep them happy and reduce both spillage and wastage

15. Filled croissants hack

Be a little experimental with your plain croissants and save yourself money on the more expensive filled bakery treats by creating your own versions.

Your kids will love to help with this too, which is why we like to do this at weekends when there is a bit more time in the mornings to make breakfast together.

And you can vary your fillings depending on what you or the children fancy that morning: strawberry jam, marmalade, chocolate spread, peanut butter – or a combination of any of the above!

★ Take a packet of plain croissants and decide what fillings you are going to use to fill them first

★ Using a medical syringe (I keep syringes from kids' used medicine bottles for this purpose) fill it with your chosen filling

★ Tear a small opening in the croissant with your fingers, or push the syringe through to make a gap in the pastry

★ Then empty the yummy filling from your syringe into your croissant

★ If you are using chocolate spread and want it a little runny, simply warm the croissant for 30–40 seconds in the microwave after filling

16. Hairbrush battle hack

They say that with children you sometimes have to pick your battles, but one contest that I feel I have won is the daily 'let me brush your hair' saga.

It's all about distraction, and the best way I have found to conquer the knots and the frizz and get their hair looking ready for the day is to wait until they are having breakfast.

★ Sit them down with their cereal-filled mugs (see Hack 14) and then brandish your weapons: hairbrush, hair bobbles, bows, clips – whatever look you want for any particular day or occasion

★ Not only will your child be distracted if there are a few overnight knots, you can French plait in peace while they get to grips with their brekkie

★ It's like a multitasking miracle and you will probably be finished around the same time

★ No more hair tantrums and fights over brushing because it will all be done without them really realising. You. Are. Welcome.

17. Ketchup bottles for milk hack

This is a great way to create independence for younger children without them (or you) crying over spilt milk.

Full milk cartons are heavy and awkward for youngsters to handle, which is why I keep old ketchup/mayonnaise or mustard bottles as my mini milk bottle versions so that children can help themselves to milk with cereal or when making a milkshake.

★ Thoroughly clean out a used ketchup bottle, or whatever type of bottle you have handy, and make sure the lid has had a good wash too

★ Fill it up with milk and pop it in the fridge, then it's ready for your child to help themselves each morning and be a bit more independent with their brekkie

★ Create your own labels with your children if you want to make them a bit more personal. You can add on the milk use-by date too if they don't get through much each day

18. Pancake muffins hack

This is a quick and adaptable food treat that can be eaten hot or cold for breakfast depending on your kids' taste buds. One bag of pancake mixture makes twelve muffins, so you will have plenty to go around or store for another day – they will keep for five days in an airtight container in the fridge. If they last that long, because they are so delicious!

★ Take a packet or bottle of pancake mixture and make it up as per the instructions

★ Take a twelve-case muffin tin and pour in the mixture so that there is an even amount in each space, with each roughly half full

★ Now you can add whatever fillings you like by putting a small selection on top of the mixture

★ I like finely chopped blueberries and strawberries, some cake decorating sprinkles or peanut butter and chocolate chips, but the possibilities are endless!

★ Pop them in the oven to cook at 175°C (345°F) for about 12–16 minutes, then remove and allow to cool down

★ They can then be placed in a container for a takeaway treat, or my children love them warmed up in the microwave (for about 12 seconds) on a plate for their breakfast

★ There are no crumbly bits or mess, which makes them easy to take out with you too. There really is 'muffin' negative to say about this hack!

MAJOR MUM
HACKS VIDEO

19. Beans and cheese toastie hack

Hot breakfasts don't need to be tricky and time-consuming – especially on school mornings when time is of the essence and seems to go quicker the slower my children put their shoes on.

The best thing about this yummy hot brekkie idea is that it doesn't have to be saved for special occasions because it's not only quick but easy – our favourite word pairing, alongside gin and tonic.

★ Take a flat bread roll or a roll that you can test will fit in your toaster

★ Make a slit in the roll and add in some grated cheese and baked beans

★ Pop the filled roll into the toaster for a couple of minutes – with the filled slit at the top (otherwise this hack won't be quick and easy but rather messy and stressful) and leave for a couple of minutes

★ When the time is up you'll have a delicious and hot breakfast toastie

MAJOR MUM
HACKS VIDEO

20. Make-ahead egg muffins hack

If you like to be prepared for the busy week ahead, this breakfast hack will be right up your organisational street because you can make these muffins ahead of time and whip them out each morning as needed.

★ Take your twelve-case muffin tray again and work out what fillings you want in your breakfast savoury treat

★ I will describe one of my faves and you can adapt according to appetite ...

★ Take a generous portion of grated cheese and baked beans – depending on how cheesy or baked-beany you like your muffins – a whisked egg and three or four slices of ham, and mix together in a bowl

★ Then pour your mixture into the muffin tray, with an even amount in each space, and bake in the oven at 175°C (345°F) for 15–20 minutes

★ Once the muffins are cooked, take them out of the tray to cool before storing in an airtight container and popping them in the fridge

★ They are now ready to be whipped out as breakfast treats for the next few days and you can spend the rest of your Sunday evening feeling smug

21. Pizza toastie hack

If the kids are demanding a pizza night but you've not got any in the freezer and you don't want to spend a fortune on a takeaway, it's time for 'pizza snack-hack made in the toaster night'! It might be a bit of a mouthful but the end product will most certainly be a mouthful of dreams.

★ Take a slice of bread and in the centre spread some tomato puree or pizza sauce so that there is a gap all the way round. If you need to make sure you aren't over-spreading, take the block cheese grater you're going to use to cut out your mini pizza shortly and place it over the top so that you know your size is right

★ Take another slice of bread and place it on top

★ Now, using the base of your cheese grater, push down fully so that the bread is cut out, discard the crust edges and, if you want to, pinch together all round the outside of your two bits of filled bread

★ Pop into the toaster for about 2 minutes and enjoy a perfect pizza toastie

22. Hidden veggie shot hack

MAJOR MUM
HACKS VIDEO

If you feel like you could negotiate a deal with the UN a lot easier than you could persuade your child to eat veggies, this hack will hopefully save a lot of stress and drama at dinner time.

Slipping these yummy vegetables unnoticed into their food when they are little means you are giving them all the good stuff but not having to face the battle that goes with it. You are welcome!

I use the following ingredients to sneak veg into a pasta dish, chilli or spag bol, and my kids have literally no idea that I've included all this good stuff.

★ Fill a baking tray with six cut-up tomatoes, three sliced courgettes, one chopped onion and four carrots (or add whatever veggies you like) cut into slices too, and bake in the oven for about 35 minutes at 200°C (390°F)

★ Once cooked, remove the veggies and put them into a blender with half a jar of passata and blend together until there are no lumps

★ Fill a cupcake baking tray, putting a couple of spoonfuls of mixture in each space, and then freeze. Once frozen, remove from the tray, place in a food bag and return to the freezer

★ These shots of goodness are then ready to be used when you want to add them to an evening meal – and no fussy eater will be any the wiser!

23. Apple rice cake hack

Plain rice cakes can be a great snack but also a little on the boring side – to look at, to chew, all-round general taste. You get my drift. Anyone else sometimes think they are munching on cardboard?

If you want your children to get a tad more excited when you whip out your packet of rice cakes for snack time, try adding some yogurt and apple on top for a fruity version that they will love!

★ Take any version of rice cake that you like – we like the supermarket own-brand ones – but make sure they are low in salt and the plain variety

★ Spread some Greek yogurt on the top so it forms a thin layer

★ Grate an apple and sprinkle the bits over the top of the rice cake, then serve with a smile

24. Mini pizza tortillas hack

Pizza nights are a big hit in our house and, although my kids love making their own versions, sometimes a big pizza portion each is too much. Which is why I love these mini versions that mean they can still be creative but there is less waste and still all the yummy taste.

★ Take a tortilla and pop it onto a baking tray

★ Spread with a generous layer of tomato puree

★ Sprinkle over a layer of cheese

★ Let your children add whatever toppings they want on top of the cheese

★ Pop the baking tray and tortilla into the oven for about 6 minutes at 180°C (356°F)

★ Remove from the oven and use a glass placed over the top to cut out small circular shapes; a circle-shaped cookie cutter will also work

★ Now you have several smaller, perfectly formed pizzas to enjoy!

25. Squirty bath toys hack

Bath time wouldn't be bath time without a rubber duckie or squirty toy added to the mix, but they can hold all sorts of yucky black mould inside them when water gets inside the hole.

What's even worse is that the black mould then gets emptied out into the lovely clean water every time your child wants to play with them in the bath. Well, no more, duckie, no more!

★ Heat up a glue gun and dry off the bath toys you want to seal – if they haven't already been contaminated with mould then they are fine to use, otherwise you might like to give them a quick clean first

★ Or buy a new set of toys and line them up

★ When the glue gun is hot, fill up the holes and leave to set

★ If you don't have a glue gun you could also use a waterproof patch or seal adhesive

★ Test out each toy to see that no water is able to enter and then you are good to go – get the bath running!

Rubber ducks come in all shapes and sizes, but their holes are usually underneath and not too big to seal. Squirty toys are obviously no longer squirty after this hack, but you also won't be contaminating your bathwater!

26. Disco bath hack

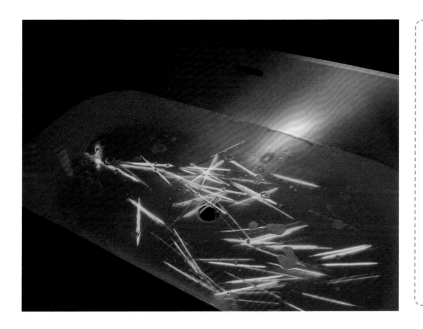

HACK THE HACK:
If your child isn't keen on having a bath, or washing hair is sometimes a battle, having a disco bath will most probably become your new bedtime routine staple – it will be getting them out of the bath that might be the problem!

Discos aren't just for an evening's entertainment and party frocks. Why not have your very own disco in the bath – no clothes required!

My children love having an impromptu disco bath and the best part of doing this watery sensory activity is that you don't need anything expensive to create it, just a pack of disposable glow sticks!

★ Fill a bath as you normally would and then take out the glow sticks – they are non-toxic and leak free, which means they are safe to use in the water

★ Break the sticks so they start to glow and then pop them in the bath

★ Turn off the bathroom lights and invite your children to step inside the disco room – formerly known as the bathroom

★ Play some music through a speaker if you want to create a real disco atmosphere, or choose some relaxation music for a more chilled vibe

★ The colours glow brighter in warm water as they react to heat, so they will make the water appear really magical

27. Frozen toy balloon hack

Another fun game that will entertain your child in the bath for hours is the frozen toy idea, where they watch their favourite toy slowly appear from its melting ice ball prison – created by you using a balloon, water and the freezer the night before.

All you need is a packet of balloons and a couple of their favourite smaller toys – small dinosaurs, little cars, little soldiers/fairies, etc.

★ Take a couple of the small toys and pop them into a balloon – two or three is usually enough, but you can add a couple more if you want

★ Fill the balloon with water and tie the end in a knot. You don't have to fill it so it's a big balloon, just enough to cover all the toys you have put in

★ Pop the balloon in the freezer and leave overnight

★ Just before bath time the next day, take the balloon out of the freezer and cut off the knotted end, then peel off the balloon and throw it away, leaving just a ball of ice and frozen toys

★ Add the frozen ball to the bath and watch as your child marvels at the ice slowly melting away to reveal their toys and the magic of science!

MAJOR MUM
HACKS VIDEO

28. Tooth brushing for under-twos hack

I've split this into two separate parts, but the aim of the hack is still the same: to help your little ones get to grips with brushing their teeth.

I know how tricky it can be to get the under-twos to brush their teeth, especially when they want to hold the toothbrush themselves but they don't always know how or what they are doing. These two hacks have really helped me.

★ Children learn a lot by watching, so next time you are brushing their teeth, make sure they are watching you, and talk with them about what you are doing

★ Give them a spare toothbrush to play with at the same time, as this will make them feel like they are part of the same activity and will give them a sense of control

★ A variation on this is to let them brush your teeth once you have finished brushing theirs

★ Keep your teeth together so they don't push the brush down your throat by accident

★ Giving them the control to brush your teeth and see what they are doing will help them when it comes to doing their own as they grow

★ As they get the hang of this, you could brush theirs and they could do yours at the same time – you'll be taking turns and making tooth brushing a staple but enjoyable part of their morning and bedtime routine

29. Toy organisation hook hack

Bath time can be lots-of-fun time with all the toys that are enjoyed with the bubbles ... but storing them all is not so easy.

And what do you do with them all when you want to clean the bath, or have a bit of a mum-soak?

★ Keeping bath toys out of the way but accessible is the key, which is why a wire basket is ideal, because it will allow the dripping-wet toys to drain

★ Take some self-adhesive sticky hooks and stick them above your bath – they should stick to tiles or the wall very easily, but make sure you dry the surface first

★ Then hang a wire basket (size can vary depending on how many toys there are) on the hooks

★ Next time your chid has finished using their toys, pop them back in the basket and let the excess water drip away through the wire mesh of the basket

30. Bubble bath modelling clay hack

This easy-to-make bubble bath modelling clay requires only a minimum number of ingredients but will add a huge amount of fun to bath time for your child.

HACK THE HACK:
This is a great summer craft idea too, and can be used in the paddling pool for hours of fun in the sun.

★ Take 80 ml of child-friendly bubble bath and mix with 1 tbsp of baby oil or melted coconut oil in a bowl

★ Decide what colour you want the modelling clay to be and mix a few drops of food colouring into the bowl. The more you add, the more the bathwater will change colour as the modelling clay dissolves, so you might want to have a lighter colour – or prefer not to add any food colouring at all

★ Add 120 ml of cornstarch depending on how efficiently the mixture thickens – you want it so thick that you can't stir it any more

★ Repeat the above steps if you want to make a collection of colours

★ Take your coloured modelling clay out of the bowl(s) and knead it on a flat surface until it's firm and doesn't stick

★ It's now ready for bath-time playing!

★ Break off small pieces at a time as they will slowly dissolve in the water, but keep any excess dough in an airtight container as it will last for a good seven days or so

MAJOR MUM HACKS VIDEO

31. Cleaning hack for building blocks and small toys

Wiping clean building blocks and small toys is a great way to keep the day-to-day germs and dirt off your children's much played with toys. Or maybe you have been given a second-hand job lot of building blocks and you want to make sure it's had a deep clean before it gets some well-deserved attention from little hands.

This is where your trusty dishwasher can come in handy – and there's you thinking it was only useful for dirty dishes!

★ Load the top drawer of your dishwasher with the toys and put it on a low-temperature wash

★ You might lose some of the stickers from the building blocks in the wash but when the rinse is done, you'll have a tray full of clean toys

★ If you have a laundry bag there isn't anything to stop you putting some building blocks in that and popping it on a quick, cool wash in your washing machine too

★ Either way you'll have clean and good-as-new building blocks and toys for your children and big kids to play with

32. Limescale remover hack for the showerhead

It's not something that is immediately obvious but once you've seen the limescale build-up on your showerhead, you can't unsee it.

But rather than add to your cleaning workload, this hack simply invites you to leave something to work its magic – and by this we mean white vinegar.

★ Take a sandwich bag – one that has tie handles – and fill it up to about a one-third full with white vinegar

★ Tie the handles carefully around the showerhead and then turn on the tap slowly so the bag fills up. You don't want the water going at full force or it will come out too quickly and the bag will come off

★ Leave the bag filled with water and vinegar tied securely around the showerhead overnight

★ Carefully untie the bag the next morning, pour away the mixture and give your showerhead a few minutes to rinse through

★ It's amazing how clean and sparkling the nozzle will now look, and, if you do this regularly, every time you step into the shower it will be as good as new!

33. Mould remover hack for bath silicone

Banish the horrible black mouldy marks around your bath and enjoy a soak in clean surroundings with this quick and simple mould-remover hack.

- ★ Put on a pair of rubber gloves and carefully pour some thick bleach directly onto the silicone around your tub – you can use an old toothbrush to brush on the bleach if that's easier

- ★ Take a roll of toilet paper and roll out five or six sheets

- ★ Roll or twist the sheets so that you have a sausage shape, and place over the silicone that you have bleached

- ★ Do this all around your bath or on areas that are covered with the yukky black stuff

- ★ Then apply some more of the bleach on top of the toilet tissue so your toilet roll sausage becomes like the filling in a bleach sandwich

- ★ Leave it for a couple of hours or ideally overnight

- ★ In the morning, pop on your rubber gloves, pull off the toilet roll and give the surface a quick wipe or rinse to reveal clean silicone underneath. Every. Single. Time.

34. Dish soap and white vinegar cleaning hack

Cleaning the bathroom is a task that doesn't fill me with any sense of excitement. Are you the same? But cleaning the bathroom quickly and efficiently – including sinks, tiles and shower doors – well, then it becomes a bit more manageable. Because no one ever said, 'Wa-hoo, let's spend the afternoon cleaning the bathroom, it will be so much fun!'

★ Take a sponge, a dish soap dispenser and some trusty white vinegar

★ Squirt equal parts of the washing-up liquid and white vinegar onto the sponge

★ Now you are ready to scrub away at all those tricky places in your bathroom without the need to spray, wait and rinse

★ This concoction also works for getting mildew off the silicone in a shower seal, meaning you'll be bathroom beautiful in a fraction of the time and with the minimum of stress

35. Rust remover with lemon hack

Stainless steel can look super clean and shiny, but keeping it that way is somewhat tricky. And if your knives and pans start to show signs of rusty stains, it can ruin the whole look of your kitchen accessories.

This hack will help you get rid of rust or harsh marks, and can also be used on your kitchen sink if needed.

- ★ Take a lemon and cut it in half
- ★ Rub the lemon half on and into the places you want to clean – sharp kitchen knives, saucepans, draining areas, etc.
- ★ Sprinkle some baking powder over where you have just rubbed the lemon and watch it bubble up
- ★ Leave for a minute then wipe clean with a damp cloth or rinse under some cold water
- ★ The surfaces should now be gleaming and you'll be able to see your smiling, satisfied face reflected back at you

36. Finger-marks hack

Inquisitive fingers like to touch, rub, feel and smother many surfaces around the house – some leave no marks whatsoever and then there are others that, well, look like they could have played a piano concerto judging by the amount of four-finger exposure.

I've found that little paw marks that are especially dirty or sweaty on stainless steel can be the trickiest to remove … until I discovered this hack.

* Take some baby oil and a cotton pad or clean cloth

* Pour a little baby oil onto your chosen cloth and pat or dab it on to the stainless steel surface with the incriminating evidence

* Rub around in a circular motion until your surface is now nice and shiny

* This hack won't stop little fingers being magnetically drawn to such a surface again, but at least you know you can make it reflection shiny without too much effort. It's a win-win!

37. Bedsock for floor mop hack

Mopping the floor on a regular basis means that you'll probably end up going through a fair few mop pads to keep your floors looking and smelling clean and fresh.

But what happens if you run out of mop heads and you find that the dog has walked mud in everywhere? That your children have decided to traipse around the kitchen and not take off their football boots? That the spillage of squash you thought you had cleared up suddenly reveals itself as the sun shines through the window? This hack will knock your socks off.

★ Ditch the mop pads and pull out a pair of bedsocks instead

★ Place a sock over the floor mount at the end of the mop handle and clean the floor as usual

★ Now instead of buying a new packet of expensive mop pads, simply pop your sock in the washing machine and reuse as often as needed

38. Dishwasher tablet for cloudy vase hack

Beautiful bunches of flowers around your house can brighten your rooms, lift your mood and add a naturally fresh fragrance to your surroundings. But I've noticed that glass vases can be left looking cloudy and stained where they're holding the water, in only a few days.

And when it's time to discard the blooms, the brownish cloudy marks are tricky to get off. Well, no more!

- ★ Take your stained vase and fill with some uncooked rice – you probably only need a cup full depending on the size of your vase

- ★ Then add some warm water, close to two-thirds full, or certainly covering the water-mark stain that needs removing

- ★ Lastly, pop in a dishwasher tablet and leave overnight

- ★ In the morning, discard all the contents and give your vase a rinse in cold water

- ★ You should now have a crystal-clear vase that looks as good as new

39. Washing-up liquid drain unblocker hack

We all know that washing-up liquid can cut through grease and dirt when you're tackling some mucky pots and pans, but this handy little liquid can also help if you find your sink is draining a little slower than normal.

It might not be a complete, permanent fix so if your sink is starting to get really blocked you might need to call in the big guns and get some heavy-duty sink unblocker, but this is a great hack for just slower-than-normal draining problems.

★ Take a big squirt of washing-up liquid and pour it down the sink

★ Leave for around 10–15 minutes

★ Now boil the kettle and pour the boiling water down the drain

★ The combination of hot water and washing-up liquid will help cut through any built-up dirt or grease in your pipes and allow them to drain more quickly and efficiently

'Here, there and everywhere', that's what I say when someone asks me where I am going, because that's what it feels like as a mum. I'm right, aren't I?

After-school clubs, play dates, swimming lessons ... sometimes it does feel like I'm mum's taxi, running my own transport line for little people, which is why it helps to be prepared. Long car journeys? Sorted. Traffic jams? Not a problem. Car sickness? It's in the bag (not literally, see Hack 45).

The key piece of advice to impart here is that journeys – on trains, in cars or on foot – don't need to be stressful if you do a little bit of prep beforehand. And then you'll find the travelling is just as fun (if not more!) than the destination.

MAJOR MUM HACKS FOR...

On The Go

40. Sandwich bag movie hack

This is the perfect way to keep your kids entertained on a long journey or if you need to break up the 'I spy' game monotony – there are only so many rounds of that I can play without wanting to bang my head against the dashboard (drama queen on board).

You will see this in my holiday plane hack too (Hack 63), but it's also ideal to use in the car.

- Take a trusty sandwich bag and lift off the front-seat headrest

- With the bag over the holes of the headrest (making sure the ziplock bit is at the bottom) push down the headrest so that it holds the bag securely when it's back in place

- You can now put your phone or tablet into the bag and press play on *Bluey*, allowing your child to watch their own screen from the comfort of their car seat without holding (we mean dropping) the phone, and you can continue driving for at least five minutes in peace

41. Bubbles and air con hack

We know there is something about a flurry of bubbles that makes toddlers go giddy with excitement (we are the same with bubbles, although they tend to be in a champers glass).

If you are with the family in slow-moving traffic and need to lighten the mood, this is a fun way to bring some giggles to the back – and maybe to the cars sat next to you in the traffic jam too.

- Keep a bottle of bubbles in the glove box so that the passenger in the front can access them when needed. You can buy multipacks of these quite cheaply from most supermarkets

- Ask the passenger (or do it yourself if you're not behind the wheel) to turn up the air con so the fan is blowing quite high

- Open up your bubble bottle, dunk the lid, then hold it in front of the blowing vent

- The bubbles will stream towards the back seat and the waiting arms and fingers wanting to pop, and you can repeat as many times as necessary or until your bubbles run out. Don't forget to replace the bottle for next time, though, otherwise those traffic queues will be filled with upset tears rather than giggles

42. Shoe organiser hack

I have found that variety is a game changer when it comes to car journeys, but if I'm driving, I don't have the capability to provide endless supplies of different activities. Which is where the simple shoe organiser comes in handy!

- Buy a couple of cheap shoe organisers that can be easily attached to the headrest of the driver's seat and/or the front passenger seat – look online if you need Velcro ones or ones with holes, depending on your car model

- Then fill them up with things that are easy to use for your kids on a car journey and that can be separated into each compartment – for example, window stickers, colouring pens and pads, a few snacks and some modelling clay

- Small drinking cups are also a perfect fit for these compartments, as are baby wipes

HACK THE HACK:
Another great storage solution that is easily accessible for little hands is a soft mesh toy bag for the window. Simply put the suction pads on each window and fill with things like sensory toys, easy-to-open snacks and a cuddly toy. For a similar idea, see Hack 50.

43. Hour-marker party bags hack

I love these 'countdown'-type hacks and you will see that I use them later on for New Year's Eve countdown ideas too. They are so versatile – you can use them in any situation that requires breaking up a long stretch of time, which makes them ideal for car or train journeys.

* Pop into a discount shop and pick up a few party favour toys; some supermarkets also do bulk-buy party bag favours

* Take whatever toys/games/activities you have bought and put them into some small brown bags – party favour bags also work well and can be cheaper to buy in bulk

* Mark each bag 'Hour 1', 'Hour 2', 'Hour 3', etc., depending on how long your car journey is, and then dish them out at each stage

* This will hopefully mean that the time countdown will be met with more of a cheer than a moan

* You could also do this in half-hour segments if you have younger children and need to break up the journey even more

44. Cereal container for rubbish hack

It's a sure fact that car footwells can collect more rubbish than the local council refuse truck ... but there is a way to keep your car mat clean and your car cleaner happy (thanks Mr Major Mum Hacks), and that's by keeping a plastic cereal container beside your front seat.

- If you have a spare cereal container that's great, but ideally you need a narrow one with a lid rather than a larger, cylindrical one. And, ideally, one with no cornflakes in it

- Pop a small bag inside as a bin liner and then tuck it neatly by the side of your seat so you can pop in sweet wrappers, tissues and snack packets, and then empty it all when you get out

45. Collapsible bowl for travel sickness hack

It's not a lot of fun feeling queasy on a long car journey. And it's even less fun when the feeling turns into actual sick. But travel sickness can strike at any time – and sometimes quite quickly – so it's always good to be prepared.

Dog water bowls or small camping washing-up bowls that collapse are ideal car travelling companions if you have any passengers that need to reach for something quicker than you can say 'bleurgh'.

* Pop one in the pocket of each door if needed, or keep them in the front. They can be bought from a variety of places, in a variety of colours and sizes

* Because they are collapsible, they fit neatly in the side of the car door and can be made into sick buckets in an instant

* Car sickness is no fun and being prepared with this hack beats the magic newspaper method they used to use at school

46. File folder for building blocks hack

Playing with building blocks can take up hours of playtime at home, which is why taking them on a long car journey or on the train seems like a fabulous idea. But how to take all the bits you need without losing a vital brick down the side of your chair or under the seat in front of you? That outcome doesn't bear thinking about ...

* You might have some of these A4 folder ring binders at home, but if not they are cheap to buy from stationery stores or supermarkets

* You need pocket folder inserts to go inside them – the ones with a popper on the top as this is where you are going to store the building blocks

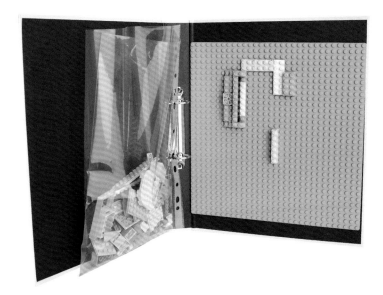

* Fill the pocket folder with building blocks

* You can add as many folders as you want, but you won't be able to fill each one with too many bricks or it won't shut

* When you've filled your folder, take some double-sided tape and attach a building blocks board to its opening flap

* Your kids now have a base to which to attach the bits they want to play with on the journey or for as long as their imagination takes them. You won't hear 'Are we there yet?' for at least five minutes

47. Art caddy for fast food hack

The wonders of the humble art caddy seem limitless, and it really comes into its own when it comes to getting a takeaway in the car. There are never enough hands to hold everything and we all want to avoid gooey chocolate milkshake all over a car seat.

* Next time you pick up a drive-through, or need an extra pair of hands when collecting a takeaway, use an art caddy instead

* Burgers and chips slot nicely into the compartments and there is always room for drinks too

48. Parking app hack to save on costs

Gone are the days when my nan would be ferreting around for 20p in her car-parking purse or my dad would be emptying his pockets for change for the meter. Parking can now be stress-free (once you find a space, of course) and relatively easy if you prepare first.

- Before you go on a day out, download an app that helps you find free or cheap parking

- Apps like this will tell you where to park for free or at lower cost, which means more ice cream money when you're out on your adventure

- If you download the parking app on your phone and register your car details they will be saved each time you use it. It will take a little bit of stress out of the day if you check your parking options when you plan your route

49. Car sticker hack

You know what it's like when you reach a destination: depending on where you go, sometimes the excitement can be too much for kids who want to get out and explore right away. And that means they sometimes forget their normal safety precautions when it comes to getting out of the car, especially in busy car parks.

My kids use this hack all the time, when I'm unpacking shopping or when we've got to the beach, for example, and I need everyone to stay in one place while I unload.

- Put a large colourful sticker on the side of your car – I put one on the side where the petrol cap flap is

- Tell your kids they all have to have a hand on the sticker while you unload what you need or get everything ready

- They can only let go of the sticker when you say and then you can all move off together

- I find this especially useful in large supermarket car parks where cars are coming and going, or at leisure centres when you have kit bags and drinks to gather up and need everyone to wait for you

50. Window toy hack

This works in the car, but I've found it's also great if you travel by train regularly or have a long rail journey coming up. If you can reserve or aim for a window seat, here are a few ideas to use the space to your advantage.

- Take with you a small bag that's filled with window activities. I go to discount shops, or you could have a look online and suss out what you want to take: window stickers or spinners, or suction toys

- If you have a big area by the window you can bring out different window toys every few minutes or, if one is particularly popular, keep the others for the return journey

- The majority of trains also have tables or aeroplane-style seat-back tables, which means you have the ideal space for cards/colouring or could even bring a small tin of modelling clay to play with

HACK THE HACK:
If you have a Harry Potter fan with you and are travelling to London King's Cross station, head for a photo opportunity at Platform 9¾!

51. Driving the trolley hack

If you need to pop into the supermarket with little ones (or you are some kind of superhuman who can do a big weekly shop with toddlers in tow, I salute you), you might find this hack a fun way to keep them entertained while you try to shop around for the best bargains.

Instead of pushing your toddler or little one around and have them facing your boring chops, spin the trolley around so they are now at the front.

- You could tell them they are now in the driving seat and have to make sure they steer the right way around the shop, while you make the most of selecting and adding all the food to the trolley

- It should be just as easy to push from the back and of course, easy to spin round again if needed

- As well as keeping your kids entertained while you grab your weekly shop, you'll probably put a few smiles on the faces of other shoppers in aisle 13 too

52. Character stickers for food hack

If you do have your little ones shop with you and you need to try to make the fruit and veg aisle a little more exciting, you will love this sticker hack. It's perfect if your kids are inclined to only want to eat bright, colourful, recognisable character-based food, as it tricks them into thinking that the healthy stuff that's good for them is fun too!

* Take a packet of their favourite stickers and, when they aren't looking, pop one or two on to food they wouldn't normally think is that exciting – a unicorn on a bunch of bananas, or a Bluey sticker on a bunch of broccoli

* Then you can ask them to find the fruit or vegetables that you have personalised and see their reaction when they realise they will be eating 'magic unicorn bananas' or Bluey's special green veg!

* You do have to be a bit sneaky with this, but it's not hard and it makes the fruit and veg aisle a lot more exciting

* Plus, you have now found a use for the million dinosaur stickers you have lying around ...

53. Potential presents picture hack

If your kids are anything like mine, I quite often get 'I want this' or 'Can I have that?' This never-ending wish list from the children is just joyful, isn't it? Not tedious at all. Not. At. All. But you can work this idea around in your favour too, because this hack not only makes it easier to remember stuff your kids might want for their birthdays, etc., after they've pointed it out one rainy Tuesday afternoon, but you can also take photos to send to relatives when they need present ideas too.

- Next time your child sees something they want to buy, take a photo of it and tell them what a great idea that is and that you will send the photo to Father Christmas or the Easter Bunny

- Then when it's Christmas and the big guy has brought them exactly what they asked for, you remind them that the photo messages must have worked!

- It's a good idea when you take these photos to keep them in a separate folder on your phone so that you can find them easily but little eyes can't

- This collection of photos is easily shown or sent to friends or relatives that might need inspiration too – you can show them exactly what the children want and exactly which shop you were in when they saw it

54. Day out photo hack (for use in emergencies)

It doesn't bear thinking about, but busy places can often mean that kids could wander out of sight and get lost in a crowd before you can shout their names like a banshee. So this is the best way to make sure that, if they do go for a wander, you are prepared.

* Before you leave for your adventure, take a full-length photo of your child, including their shoes

* In case they do wander off in a busy/unfamiliar place and you start to panic and your mind goes blank, you have a photo on your phone all ready to show people exactly what your child looks like and what they are wearing, so everyone can be scanning and looking for them

* Another good tip to remember is that if you ever do lose your child, instead of shouting their name, shout out what they are wearing – for example, boy, blond hair, red top, navy shorts, missing. Keep repeating it as many times as needed, so that people can look for a child fitting that description and wearing that clothing

55. Wristband number for missing children hack

Lots of places give you and your child wristbands to wear, to acknowledge you have paid to be in the attraction or maybe because there's a time limit for the activity.

But these are also good accessories to add an extra layer of security if you're in a soft-play area, for example, and you get separated from them.

- I always carry a permanent marker in my bag so that I can write my phone number on the band before I pop it on my child's wrist

- If the two of you ever get separated there is an easily identifiable number someone can call right away

- Alternatively, you can write your phone number on their arm with a normal pen, just in case

0123456ϯ

56. Plasters and cash in phone case hack

Your mobile phone case is a handy storage place to keep extra essentials for when you don't want to carry around a mountainous bag with you – sometimes all you need is money and a few first-aid items.

- I always carry a bit of cash in the back of my phone case for the 'just in case' moments when I'm out and I might need cash. I know that's a bit old-fashioned and you can pay at most places with your phone wallet accounts, but you'd be surprised how many places won't take a card

- I also have a child that falls down a lot, so I've found that keeping one or two plasters in the back of my phone is also vital and can turn a disastrous meltdown situation into one that is taken care of quite quickly. And it's even better if they are colourful children's plasters too – they seem to dry the tears a lot quicker

Spring is such an exciting time isn't it? It feels like we've all come out of a winter hibernation and nature wants to join in the celebration by showcasing beautiful blossom on the trees, daffodils and crocuses everywhere you look. The smell of cut grass, watching the butterflies and the bees and listening to the birds – this time of year really does put a smile on my face. And I love summertime too – a period of chilled picnics, fun in the sun, water fights and BBQs, lots of ice creams and time spent playing endlessly outside.

I want you to enjoy everything you love about the spring and summer sun-filled days, and I want to share with you ways that I hope will help – whether that's hacks for flying away on your hols or quick and simple recipes to help take the stress out of springtime picnics or sizzling summer BBQs.

Above all, I want you to enjoy those sun-kissed moments with your kids and give yourself time to enjoy a summer mocktail or cocktail or two while you do. Cheers, m'dears!

Spring/Summer

57. Wardrobe cube/shoe organiser hack

Working out what clothes of your own you need to take on holiday can be hugely stressful, but then trying to pack for small children as well involves more brain work than necessary. Let this hack lighten your mental load!

★ A wardrobe cube or an over-the-door shoe rack will become your new packing pal as you can use each compartment for an outfit

★ Wardrobe cubes usually have five spaces, so if you're going for a short break put all the children's outfits in a separate cube for each day

★ If you are going for a longer holiday you can use each compartment to keep all T-shirts together, all nightwear together, all swimwear together, etc.

★ Over-the-door hangers are great for the same reason – they usually have rows of two, three or four, which is a great help in organising for my four children. Again, each outfit can go into a separate compartment and then the whole thing rolled easily into a suitcase

★ When you arrive at your holiday home or hotel, you can just unravel the organiser and hang it up – all outfits for each child for each day of the hols are ready to go!

★ And because there is zero unpacking, you'll have more time for holiday cocktails. Cheers!

58. Squash and drinking water hack

When you are doing your holiday destination research, make sure you check whether you can drink the local tap water. This is a huge game changer as I see so many people on holiday in supermarkets packing bottles and bottles of mineral water in their trollies when the tap water is completely safe to drink!

★ My first point is to check whether the local drinking water is safe and save yourself a fortune if it is – tap water is tap water. And it's free!

★ If it is safe, don't forget to pack your water bottles too, so that every time you head out you can refill as you go

★ If your children are a tad fussy over the taste of water, or prefer squash, you don't need to buy them expensive squash in restaurants either, simply take a small squeezy concentrated juice with you and add it to their water

59. Buggy fan hack

Scheduled nap times can sometimes go out the window when you're on holiday, which means that buggies and prams become the ideal portable place for a snooze when you're out and about. But it's tricky when you want to watch older kids enjoy themselves and you're worried about the little ones getting too hot.

★ Have a look online before you depart for portable fans that can attach onto buggies and prams – there are lots to choose from, depending on your budget

★ If you already have some handheld ones at home take them with you, along with some cable ties to help you attach them

★ Now when you are by the pool and your child is napping you know that they will stay cool in the breeze from the fan

★ Pack a few extra batteries to make sure you have plenty, and relax … that holiday book won't read itself!

60. Silicone cupcake holder for drinks hack

Holidays and daily ice lollies go hand in sticky hand. But sticky hands and ice cream juice on clothes aren't a lot of fun. And because lollies melt even quicker in the hot holiday sun, you'll be going through a packet of baby wipes quicker than you can say, er, pass me another baby wipe.

To stop the icky-sticky wetness of an ice cream lolly getting all over your kids' fingers, hands and clothes, try taking some silicone cupcake cases on your hols too.

★ Taking a packet of silicone cupcake cases – as many as you have children – make a slit in the bottom of each case, not very long but in the centre

★ You'll then be able to put the cases on the ends of ice lollies to stop the stickiness dribbling down the stick and onto little hands – everything goes into the case

★ You can also use them to put over the top of a child's cup and pop a straw through the top. It's like a giant umbrella over the juice and the cupcake case will stop any little bugs flying into the liquid. Because, let's face it, meltdowns over flies in squash is a holiday tantrum we can all do without

61. Vacuum-packing nappies hack

Saving space in your luggage is one of those things that make you feel like you are winning at life (the little wins make all the difference), but what to do with bulky nappies that take up a lot of precious space?

- ★ If you haven't got any vacuum bags at home, have a look online or at the supermarket for some that fit your budget and needs

- ★ These super space savers can now be used for nappies – they will shrink to next to nothing and give you a whole lot more packing space

- ★ We use vacuum bags for a variety of things – they are especially useful when you are going camping because once you've packed the tent, the chairs and all the sleeping gear in the boot of your car, you don't have a lot of space for anything else. But, thanks to your vacuum bags, you can pack your entire wardrobe if you need to!

HACK THE HACK:
Now that you've gained a little more space in your holiday suitcase, make sure you pack some beach toys – buckets and spades, etc. – to save you buying hugely expensive ones on holiday. Buckets can be packed inside one another and filled with socks or something else useful, and you will be able to slide in a couple of spades quite easily too. More ice cream money!

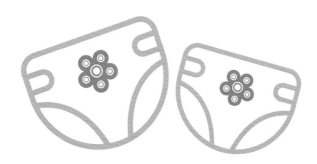

62. Beach picnic hack

Eating out on holiday can be an expensive business, and while you might budget for evening meals at restaurants, if you are feeding a large family at lunchtime in a café too, the holiday pennies quickly disappear!

But there is a way of enjoying the local produce without spending a fortune on a sit-down meal every time. Here's how …

★ It's all about being prepared. When you go to the beach, check out what local bakeries or supermarkets are nearby

★ Always take some cutlery out with you, especially a bread knife and some napkins or paper plates in a cool box

★ When it's lunchtime, pop into the local bakery and grab yourself a baguette or rolls – or, if you prefer, ready-made sandwiches – to eat on the beach

★ You'll find cheaper baguette fillings in the local supermarket too – cheese and ham or salami, for example – and you can then head back to the beach and make up your own picnic feast for half the price of a café lunch

63. Sandwich bag phone holder hack

If you're doing a short-haul flight where there will be no inflight entertainment to watch, make your own little cinema screen with a phone and a sandwich bag.

★ It's always handy to download a film or a couple of episodes of your child's favourite show before you start a long journey. Watching films over flaky Wi-Fi is probably a cause of high blood pressure among most preschool parents, so my advice is to always download before you go

★ Take a clear sandwich bag and pop your phone or tablet inside. Then, tuck the bag behind the still-stowed tray table and your child has their own little TV screen completely hands-free

★ This also works brilliantly on long car journeys (see Hack 40)

64. Passport sticker hack

I like to think I'm very organised when it comes to travelling because, well, I have to be – I have four kids to keep track of and keep tickets/passports/ documents for. Passport covers used to be my go-to when it came to distinguishing whose passport was whose when it was just my husband and me, but that cost can add up when you have another four to buy. And passport control don't like you having passports in covers so it just meant I ended up carrying them too. Which, you know, is just what you need at an airport isn't it, more to carry!

★ Instead of having a frantic flick through each passport to match the right photo with the right person (we've usually lost the will by the end of it all) simply add a sticker to each one

★ 'A sticker!' I hear you cry. 'Can it really be that simple?' Yes it can, my friends, yes it can

★ You might already have some cheap, colourful stickers at home, but you can go for any that suit your children – princess, teddies, horses, etc. Get your child to choose one and that is theirs to remember

★ Stick the chosen design onto the back of all the passports, avoiding the corners as I find they can catch and peel off more quickly if placed there

65. Plane boarding hack

I know there is usually priority boarding for families with young children, and I also understand that you might have a child that likes to settle themselves on the plane and get used to their surroundings to help them with the flight.

But this is a great 'don't feel you have to rush' hack for those of you that travel with toddlers.

★ There is always a huge urge to get on the plane, to be first in the queue, to board as quickly as you can. But then if your toddler or preschooler suddenly decides to have a tantrum for no reason, you will be stuck in a confined space trying to calm down an upset little one while other people are still boarding and you still have time to wait before take-off. No one wants to lengthen tantrum time … and you won't be making any friends on the plane either!

★ My advice? Take the least stressful option and wait. And then wait some more. Join the queue at the end. You'll still be sitting down and ready for take-off in plenty of time, but won't need to spend ages entertaining a toddler before the plane even starts taxiing

HACK THE HACK:
Make sure your children have walked around the airport at least fifteen times (a joke, but you get the gist) before you board. The key is to get their little legs all tired and ready for a sit-down or, ideally, a rest on the plane. Wander with them, limit sitting down/buggy time and get those muscles moving so everyone is ready for a good sit-down and chill when you finally board

EXTRA HACK:
Once you board the plane and are all strapped in, you might notice that your small child loves playing with their own seat belt – which puts cabin crew on full safety alert. Simply ask for a spare seat belt for them to play with. It might only keep them entertained for ten minutes or so but should get you through take-off and landing. It's the small wins!

66. Food and drink ear-popping hack

Keeping your toddler entertained during take-off and landing to distract them from the noise and their ears popping is key to keeping everyone happy – painful ears do not a happy traveller make.

★ Always encourage your child to have something to eat or drink when taking off and landing

★ It doesn't need to be a 'sucky' sweet – you don't want to have a choking hazard on your hands if your child is too little to understand

★ Dry snacks are a great way to stay mess free and to get them chewing to limit painful ears – take with you a collection of crisps, wafers, rice cakes and dried raisins to chew on

★ You could create a 'snack box' just for them – fill each compartment with a different snack and let them choose. A bit like a busy box (see the next hack) but smaller – these are available online in a variety of colours and sizes

67. Individual busy box hack

Finding ways to keep kids entertained on a flight is probably the thing I get asked about the most. I have found that there is no one thing that magically makes time disappear (soz), but I have found lots of ways for everyone on the plane to benefit from quiet toddlers.

★ Look online or in discount shops on the high street for a lunchbox that has a few compartments

★ Now you can fill these with bricks, some magnetic blocks and a few fidget spinners, to while away the time and flying miles

★ Sorting and putting stuff back into the little boxes is another good time-consuming activity too

★ If your child is particularly into building blocks, you can create a travel folder too (see Hack 46)

68. Child's rucksack hack

We've mentioned quite a few ideas and activities to keep your little ones busy on the plane, but where to put it all? Did you know that each child can have their own little rucksack as their own bag allowance? That means you can get them to carry their bits, and have all their games and snacks in their own bag.

★ The fun can start when you organise all the bits you have ready for them to have on the plane or on your travels and pack the bag together

★ They can then be a bit more independent and pack for themselves, and they will know exactly what's in their bag for when they are sitting down and cruising at 30,000 feet

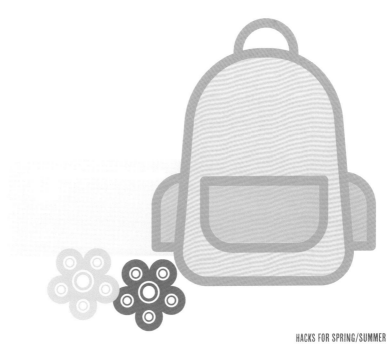

69. Pop-up laundry basket for the beach hack

Pop-up laundry baskets can serve many purposes around the house (toys, clothes, laundry, etc.), but because they are quick to flatten down and lightweight to carry around, they are also your beach best friend.

★ Set out your picnic blanket and pop out your laundry basket

★ Fill it with beach towels for everyone so they are all in one place, or pop in the toys that the kids wanted to take with you

★ The other good thing about laundry baskets is that they are quite often mesh designs, which means you can pack everything back in there at the end of the day, give it a good shake before you leave the beach and you will be able to keep your hotel or villa sand-free

70. Beach towel clutch hack

If you are fed up with rummaging around in your beach bag trying to find goggles for one child or looking for your other child's sunnies, you'll know it's a never-ending scramble to match the right item with the right child.

Well, let me show you a clever little way of keeping everything together – sunglasses, goggles, swimwear – all within their own beach towel, which is easy to carry. Prepare to be amazed!

★ Start by folding the towel on the longer side once and then over again and then bring the other long side and fold it in – folding it into thirds basically

★ Then fold up the bottom section of the towel so it's about a third of the way up – this creates the pocket

★ Now put all that your child will need in the middle, then roll the top of the towel downwards to meet the fold

★ Then all you need to do is tuck this part into the pocket and you have a pillow-like shaped clutch bag for your child to carry to the beach

MAJOR MUM
HACKS VIDEO

71. Sun cream application hacks

Is anyone else still traumatised by the memory of having their suntan lotion smothered on liberally and forcefully by overzealous parents when all you wanted was to run into the sea? And you'd probably taste suntan lotion for a week afterwards, such was the thickness and potency of the cream. We don't like to be dramatic, but it was pretty traumatic! Luckily, with these three hacks, our kids don't have to go through the same excitement.

★ Use a fake tan mitt to apply sun cream onto the kids' bodies – this is softer for them, and helps spread the cream into all the nooks and crannies evenly and smoothly

★ Using a make-up sponge is perfect for the face – it's a game changer and will stop the cries of 'Eurgh, Mum, you've got it in my eyes!' A make-up sponge allows for easy application across the face without slapdash slathering – your children will thank you

★ SPF powder for hairlines: sprinkle some of this sunscreen powder along the edge of your kid's hairline and avoid stickiness in their hair that is tricky to get off

HACK THE HACK:

If you're worried about forgetting when it's next time for a suntan lotion top-up, simply use a black marker pen to note on your suntan lotion bottle the time you put it on, then you'll have a visual reminder of the last time of application. Alternatively, you can make a list of times that you want to apply and tick them off as you go during the day.

72. Dog swimming pool at the beach hack

There are a huge variety of pop-up dog swimming pools on offer for your four-legged friends to use, but I have found they are also ideal for little ones to use on the beach.

This is perfect if you've got an age gap between your kids – your older ones want to paddle, but your little ones want to stay further up the beach, so you can create your own mini beach right next to you for them.

★ Select a suitable dog paddling pool to buy – we opt for these rather than mini paddling pools as they are usually foldable rather than inflatable and have higher sides to keep the water in

★ Fill up with water you've fetched with sandcastle buckets from the sea, and enjoy letting your little ones have their own private beach-side pool

★ They'll be able to splash and keep cool under your watchful eye and you can keep them in the shade of your beach umbrella too

73. Pebble painting and sand art hack

I'm always coming up with ways to combine an activity with a way of savouring an activity because so much of what we do for our children is to make memories with them – a keepsake of an occasion seems like the ideal way to tick all boxes.

I am also always trying to find ways of creating nice personal mementos for grandparents, and the beach provides lots of art supplies for just that!

★ Take some watercolour paints, fill a bucket with water and ask your kids to paint some stones for Granny

★ If you want to bring paper they can also use that to create their masterpiece sea-view artwork for Grampy

★ And if you want to take some glue, you can pop a bit on their hands and then press them on to a piece of paper. Wash the glue off their hands and get them to sprinkle sand all over the paper to reveal where their little paw prints are! Nanny and Pop Pops will love this

74. Hairdryer/air pump hack

The thought of blowing up a swimming pool by lung power alone is enough to leave it way back in the shed with the comment 'Sorry kids, can't seem to find it!' Or maybe you have a foot pump but don't fancy your calves being given an enthusiastic workout.

Go inside, grab your hairdryer instead and follow carefully ...

★ Cut the top half off an empty plastic water or lemonade bottle – the one-litre size rather than the smaller ones – and pop the bottom half in the recycling bin

★ Put the half-bottle over the end of the hairdryer and stick around the edges with strong tape – you don't want to let out any air so you may need to wrap it around a few times

★ The resulting contraption will act like an air pump so you should now be able to blow air into any inflatable you wish – simply put the hairdryer onto a cool setting and the nozzle of the bottle onto the valve of paddling pool and you're off!

MAJOR MUM
HACKS VIDEO

75. Chalk paint for pavement art hack

If your kids are anything like mine, they love drawing with chalk in the summer on the patio. Or on the pavement outside. Or the walls. But you can turn that chalk into chalk paint very easily, which makes it even more fun to use.

- ★ Fill an empty ice cream tub or bowl with water and take it outside

- ★ Simply soak the chalk – the chunkier the better – in water and then encourage your kids to get painting with the chalk

- ★ You might want to soak the chalk for a while before use. Alternatively, you could soak it in a container overnight, which will mean its ready to paint with the next day if your kids want to use some paintbrushes instead

- ★ Look out Damien Hirst, there are some new kids on the block!

76. Reusable sponges water fight hack

I loved water fights when I was younger, much like my kids do now, but the constant use of the tap and the fiddliness of the balloons means that water fights end up being one big water mess plus a lot of broken balloons and frustrated kids.

But I've come up with a much easier water fight hack that doesn't require any fiddly little balloon tying and helps cool everyone off on hot summer days.

★ Take a couple of flat kitchen sponges – the basic colourful cellulose ones you can get from the supermarket in the cleaning aisle

★ Each sponge 'balloon' requires two sponges so take one at a time and cut each sponge into four strips, then eight strips, and then tie them together in the middle with an elastic band.

★ Continue cutting and tying as many sponge balloons as you need. The good thing is that they can be used and reused as many times as needed, and you don't need to go around and pick up little bits of popped balloon

★ Fill a bucket with water and drop the sponges in so they are pre-soaked and ready to be thrown. Let the fun begin!

77. Cable tie bubble hack

There is nothing that provokes squeals of delight like kids blowing bubbles and then watching excitedly as they travel up into the sky.

And there is nothing that provokes screams and tears of upset like the same kids dropping the bubble mixture and watching it dribble out all over the floor. My hack will help you avoid this pain!

★ Bubble mixtures in long tubes can be easily attached to things like a garden chair, table legs or a fence panel with a cable tie or strong sticky tape

★ This keeps the tube of mixture upright, allowing your kid to take out the wand and enjoy blowing out their bubbles and running around chasing them

★ Then, every time they need a re-dunk, the mixture is safely secured and ready for them. It's like the weight of the world has been lifted from your shoulders, right?

78. Garden twister hack

Games in the garden are a lot of fun, but you don't need to buy expensive options – creating your own unique version is just as effective for play. Plus, you can have an extra game when it comes to making and creating it too!

Twister is one of our favourite games to play and it's very simple to recreate for the grass.

- ★ Take a piece of A4 paper and cut a huge circle in it
- ★ If you don't have any semi-permanent paint you could use temporary hair colour spray instead
- ★ Using the paper as a template, spray circles on your lawn in the style of a Twister board
- ★ Now let the paint dry, get out the Twister spinner and get spinning!

79. Outside movie night hack

Winter movie nights when you're snuggled inside under a duvet are great fun. But there is something super special about watching a movie on a summer evening, chilling outside as the stars come out. It's just pure magic. The good news is you don't have to spend a fortune on movie equipment or hiring specialist projectors, Major Mum Hacks Movie Nights is here to help.

★ Have a look online for smartphone projectors. You can usually get them for around £30 or less

★ Take a white king-size bed sheet and hang it up outside, either on a fence or over a football goal – wherever you have space in your garden

★ Take an empty inflatable pool and add lots of snuggly cushions and blankets. You could set this up on a picnic blanket, but I've found keeping everyone contained in an empty pool is quite fun

★ Now all you need to do is grab the popcorn, turn on the projector and press play on your phone!

★ I love having lots of movie nights over the summer – I have movie theme nights and snacks, and really go to town. And why not get your children to invite their friends over for the Casey Cinema Experience – no tickets required!

80. Chocolate bar and fruit fondue hack

Summer picnics are, in the words of Tina Turner, 'simply the best' and turn normal sandwiches, fruit and crisps into far more exciting lunches because you are outside and enjoying the fresh air. But puddings can be a little bit tricky because anything chocolatey just seems to melt – which is exactly what you want for this hack!

* ★ Take a large bar of plain chocolate and open it out so it's sitting in the sun

* ★ Depending on how warm it is, after about 10–15 minutes it will have melted

* ★ Now hand out the strawberries or any other fruit you want to use and get dipping!

* ★ Now you have your very own summer chocolate fondue!

* ★ Bring marshmallows and some sticks if you want to keep hands free of chocolate stickiness, or simply lick your fingers for added delight

81. Muffin tray for drink spills hack

Paper cups and jugs are a great way of keeping everyone happy and hydrated, but I always find that no matter how careful I am, I end up knocking over or spilling drinks when I'm out for a picnic or on the beach. I don't like to think of myself as clumsy, but there are times …

This hack helps stop the cups – and, more importantly, the liquid in the cups – from spilling over, and keeps everyone happy.

- ★ Ever noticed that muffin trays are the ideal size for carrying cups? No? Well, let me tell you, they are perfect

- ★ Pack a small muffin tray in with the picnic bag and you'll have a stable base in which to leave cups of juice for kids and adults

- ★ No spills, no upsets, no need for tears

- ★ Some muffin trays are suitable for holding smaller cans of pop too – another favourite of mine to spill

82. Crisp packet bowl hack

I often like to take a sharing-size bag of crisps to a picnic or to the beach – the larger bags are often cheaper and there is less waste to dispose of. But it only takes one excitable grab for the bag to go over, sending crisps all over the place. One sure way to stop this happening is to turn the packet into a bowl.

★ Take your bag of crisps and open carefully so you don't rip it and the packet opens fully

★ Holding the packet upright, carefully push up the crisps from the bottom and, using both hands, you fold in the edges of the bottom of the packet in a circle shape

★ Continue doing this until you have a solid base and the crisps are at the top of your new bowl

★ Now fold down the top edges of the top of the crisp packet to make it neat and, hey presto, your snack-hack bowl is ready!

MAJOR MUM
HACKS VIDEO

83. Yogurt drink in a cup hack

I've already mentioned the benefits of taking cupcake cases out with you on holidays to protect your cups of juice being swamped by little bugs or flies (see Hack 60). But I've also found yogurt drinks can be tricky for little drinkers to not spill everywhere. If you're like me and you don't like to cry over spilt yogurt drinks, this hack is going to help.

* ★ If your child has a drinks bottle that has a straw section attached to the lid you will love this

* ★ Instead of peeling off the lid of the yogurt drink, pierce the lid of the yogurt drink with the straw bit of your drinks container and push down

* ★ Now put the lid, the straw and the yogurt drink into the rest of the drinks bottle – no fuss, no mess, and they can carry around their drink without you panicking about spills

84. Apple elastic band hack

My kids love apples when we're out on a picnic, but they prefer to have them cut up as a snack. It's a bit of a faff to take a knife with you to do this so I always pre-cut at home to save time and effort. 'But don't the bits go brown?' I hear you cry. Not if you follow the Casey way!

★ Cut your apples using an apple slicer in the normal way at home, but don't go right to the bottom

★ Bring the pieces back all in together and secure the apple with an elastic band or hair bobble (whatever you have most of lying around)

★ Pop the apple in the fridge with the rest of your picnic goodies and then when it's time to enjoy at the picnic, the slices will be ready to hand out and enjoyed

★ Or if your little ones don't want it after all, you have ready-made slices for your summer mocktail or cocktail. I never like to waste things in my house!

85. Picnic flask hacks

A flask isn't just for tea and coffee, oh no, my friends. Lots of you love this hack as much as I do and know what a life (and sanity) saver it is. But for those of you not sure, let me just say that a humble flask makes for the best food container in the world.

★ Flasks can be used for hot or cold snacks. We'll start with hot. If you want hotdogs as a picnic treat, take an empty flask and pour boiling water into it

★ Cook some hot dog sausages in the microwave or on the stove and then remove the water from the flask and replace with the cooked sausages

★ When you are ready to eat on your picnic, your sausages will still be warm and ready to be added to some pre-cut rolls

★ For pudding or for an ice cream snack, take another empty flask and pop it in the freezer for a couple of hours before you are due to head out. Then just before you leave, add in the ice lollies and pop on the flask lid. Mini twisters work well, as do small juice lollies. As well as saving you a fortune on ice creams when you're out, you won't have to wait in any long queues when your kids are hot and bothered and need a cooling lolly

★ We've said it before and we'll say it again, flasks … flipping love 'em!

86. Watermelon ice lollies hack

I call these watermelon lollies even though kiwis, blueberries and yogurt are in the recipe too – but that's a bit of a mouthful isn't it?

This is a great breakfast alternative in the summer and one that feels like a sneaky treat too. Plus, it will help keep the kids cool on a hot summer morning. Or simply serve as a nice cooling after-school snack.

★ Take some ice lolly moulds from the freezer

★ Cut up and blitz some watermelon in a food processor, then fill up your lolly moulds until they are just under halfway full

★ Add a handful of blueberries, then place in the freezer for 10 minutes

★ While they are freezing, blitz a couple of kiwi fruits too

★ Take the lollies from the freezer, add a couple of spoonfuls of yogurt on top and then the blitzed kiwi on top of that

★ Add lolly sticks into the mix and then return to the freezer for a few hours. These yummy treats will be ready and waiting for you when you want them!

MAJOR MUM
HACKS VIDEO

87. Watermelon and berry jelly hack

If you love the watermelon ice lollies (see previous hack), then you'll love this just as much. It's a fun way to serve and eat jelly, and makes good use of all the watermelon.

MAJOR MUM HACKS VIDEO

* ★ Get a good-sized watermelon and cut off the top

* ★ Scoop out the contents – which you can use for the previous hack too (I am good to you, aren't I?!)

* ★ Now pop into the empty watermelon shell fruits such a strawberries, raspberries, kiwis and blueberries

* ★ In a separate jug, mix up some jelly as directed on the packet, but don't add any cold water at this stage

* ★ Add a sachet of gelatine powder to the jelly and stir well, then add in the required amount of cold water

* ★ Pour the jelly into the watermelon, over the fruit, and pop it all in the fridge to set for a minimum of seven hours

* ★ This is great to be left overnight so that in the morning – or whenever you are ready to eat it after the setting period – you can cut the watermelon into segments and enjoy

88. Cereal lolly for breakfast hack

Somehow starting the day with a lolly means breakfast is a lot more fun than it is in winter – who wouldn't want to wake up with a frozen snack up for grabs? Besides, it makes a change from a bowl of cereal, doesn't it?

★ Take out your trusty ice lolly moulds and add in cereal of your choice – I find colourful fruit hoops or something similar works well and my kids love them

★ You probably want to aim for three-quarters of the lolly mould full of cereal and then add some natural or vanilla yogurt on top

★ Put the moulds in the freezer and leave overnight. Now you when your kids wake up you can say to them it's lollies for breakfast – a dream come true, right?! And a nice stress-free breakfast time for all.

MAJOR MUM
HACKS VIDEO

89. Frozen yogurt disc hack

If your kids like a cool breakfast on a summer morning, then they'll love these – they really are, er, cool. They combine all the ingredients that work together well and can be adapted to include the little extras that your child enjoys. No simple bowl of cereal can do that, eh?

★ These are ideally prepared the night before, so get your kids to help you as a pre-bedtime activity

★ Take a tub of yogurt – you can choose Greek, vanilla, natural or whatever flavour you prefer

★ Take a baking tray and cover it with baking paper, then spoon a couple of dollops of yogurt onto the paper so you have about six disc shapes

★ Pop on top some granola or a handful of your favourite cereal, then you can add some sauce or honey for an extra topping treat, or some fresh fruit – add whatever you want or make a selection

★ You can now put them in the freezer overnight for a frozen treat in the morning, or keep them for another time – they last up to two months in the freezer, so they can be enjoyed all summer!

MAJOR MUM
HACKS VIDEO

Autumn and winter can be a stressful time of year: not only are you faced with getting the school routine organised, there seems to be a never-ending cycle of runny noses, coughs, colds and rainy days, all combined with fewer daylight hours. This time of year can make you want to hibernate and hunker down with a hot chocolate under the duvet and not move until spring! If only your excitable and cooped-up children would get that message!

But, fear not, here is a collection of some of my favourite autumn and winter hacks to help navigate what can be a fraught and emotional time, but is one also filled with autumnal excitement, frosty fun and winter magic.

MAJOR MUM HACKS FOR...
Autumn/Winter

90. Sticky notepad back to school hack

You might have a child who is particularly nervous about going back to school after the holidays, and while some kids don't want to think about it until the day before, I have found this hack helps those who need that bit more control over their routine. It's simple, it's easy and visual – what's not to love?!

* Ask your child when they think they might want to start their back to school countdown. It could be a week before the end of the hols – or more or less – whatever time they think they need

* Get some sticky notes or a magnetic notepad for the fridge and write on the corresponding number of days – so if you are doing a week countdown, say, write 7 in the middle of one page or note, 6 on the next, etc.

* Each day, let them rip off the notepad page or take down the sticky note as a visual exercise that will help them feel more in control when school time starts

HACK THE HACK:
Another good tip to ease them back into the school mindset so that it's not too much of a huge change, is to get their bedtime and wake-up routine back to 'school settings' a week before the end of the hols. It will help them transition from lazy summer evenings and get their body clocks back on track.

91. Restock pencil case hack

My children always seem to be losing pens or erasers either at school or out of their pockets or bags, and it's sometimes hard to keep track of what extra supplies I need to get.

Just as I would keep organised supplies for most areas at home, I like to make sure I have everything available for ease so I'm not faced with 'Mum, I need a new protractor for my test' first thing on a Monday morning.

- ⭐ Art caddies come to the rescue once again (I should have shares in these bad boys). You can find them cheaply online or at local craft stores depending on what size you want

- ⭐ Stock up on stationery supplies in discount stores or at supermarkets – most places have items to buy in bulk, which is cheaper and perfect for what you need here

- ⭐ Pop all your supplies in the art caddy – pens, pencils, rulers, sharpeners – and do a weekly reminder for your kids to restock their pencil cases – I do this on a Friday so their bags can be put away ready for after the weekend

92. Term-time clock hack

School-day routines can become distant memories in the lazy, carefree days of summer. Even a week off at half-term can throw the morning and evening school-day routine off-kilter – which, of course, is as it should be. But I have a clever way to help your child get back on track and also be aware of times of the day, so they know what is happening when. My kids love to know what we're doing after this or after that … and now they can have a visual clue too.

* Buy a cheap clock and get some coloured pens

* Colour in sections of the clock to indicate that you want your kids to know when it's time for something – I usually colour in a section between homework and bedtime, for instance

* Then take a piece of paper and mark on it a key to the colours you've used on the clock – for example, homework (green), play (purple), dinner (dark blue), family time (red), bath (light blue), brush teeth (white), story time (orange), bedtime (pink)

* Stick this next to the clock – you could put it in a cheap frame if you want to keep it safe – and explain to your kids what all the colours mean

* Now your kids only need to look at the clock to find out what they're doing when, and won't have to keep asking you. Result!

93. Grab-and-go lunchbox hack

A grab-and-go lunchbox does two things that will make your life easier – because you can get everything prepared in advance, you can put it away until needed, and you are also giving your kids a great sense of control because they can choose what they want to put in their lunchbox in the mornings.

* Take four large containers and number them 1, 2, 3 and 4. It's then a case of preparing everything your kids will need for a few days to make up their lunchboxes

* In box number 1 you could add some sandwiches or wraps

* In box number 2 add in some dairy, so cheese strings or cut-up cheese and yogurt – they can choose two of these

* In box number 3 add some fruit – bananas, pre-cut apples or some cut grapes. They can choose two of these

* Finally, in box number 4 you can add some savoury biscuits or crisps – they can choose one of these

* Your kids will feel independent about making good choices for their lunchbox and you can then put everything back in the fridge to bring out again the next day

HACK THE HACK:
Make your own kids mini snack pack with ham and cheese as another option and variation for lunchboxes. Put out mini crackers, cut up some ham and cheese into circles and invite your kids to help themselves.

94. Left foot/right foot sticker hack

If you have younger children that need a bit of help with knowing their left from their right foot, and which shoe to put on which foot (it's a confusing business, you know), I have a simple solution for all your shoe-selecting little ones – stickers!

★ Take a sticker that is large enough for them to see and then cut it in half

★ Stick one half inside on the insole of one shoe and the other half in the other shoe

★ Now every time your child gets changed for PE or something at school, they will know that if they place their shoes the correct way round the sticker picture looks complete – it won't if the shoes are the wrong way round

★ You can try this with name stickers too, putting their first name in the left shoe and last name in the right, if they are a little older but still want a bit of reassurance

★ It's a great way to encourage independence – those shoes are made for walking!

95. Art caddy getting ready hack

This is the perfect hack to help your child focus on their morning routine while also giving them a bit of independence over their own self-care too. And because repeating the phrase 'Have you brushed your teeth and combed your hair?' a million times each morning is something we love to do, said no mum ever!

⭐ Use a three-sectioned art caddy and number the sections 1, 2 and 3 with a coloured pen, or use number stickers if you have them

⭐ Pop a toothbrush and some toothpaste in section 1 to remind them to brush their teeth as their first step (you could also add a little two-minute egg timer to help them know how long to brush)

⭐ Then their flannel and some soap goes in section 2 to remind them to wash their hands and face

⭐ In number 3 you can put a hairbrush, some hair ties, accessories or hair gel so they can finish off their own look for the day

⭐ As your child gets older you can adapt this hack by using the space for vitamins, suntan lotion, lip balm, etc.

HACK THE HACK:
This hack also works brilliantly for bedtime routines and you can slot a favourite bedtime read into their final section too. There are numerous caddy colours and styles available (we absolutely love these in our house) and the independence this gives kids over their own routines is great.

96. Washable markers for window art hack

Drawing and colouring activities are always fun, but can be tedious if you are forever running out of spare card or coloured paper.

So to make art time more exciting for your kids, give them a box of washable marker pens and tell them to use the windows instead!

★ Repeat as many times as necessary that this activity is only for glass windows and glass doors and NOT the walls, or set them down in front of the patio doors, for example, so you can keep an eye on them in one place

★ Ask them to decorate or draw on the glass in front of them – no paper required!

★ Let their imaginations run riot or set them some challenges: can they make stained-glass window patterns or draw a racetrack for rain droplets?

★ Now pop the kettle on and have a sit-down with a coffee while they work on their masterpieces

★ Once they are finished, cleaning the windows can be just as fun. Give them a damp cloth and get them to wipe away their drawings. You can go over this later for a proper clean of course, but it's a fun way to get them to keep an activity going if you haven't quite finished your cuppa

97. Fort-making hack

Building forts doesn't need to be an outside activity where you spend hours in the woods with your children finding and collecting sticks for the perfect lookout den.

When the weather is rubbish outside but they still like the idea of creating their own fort, just raid your laundry cupboard for some materials!

* Clear a floor space in the room best suited for your inside camp

* Take some bed sheets and blankets, and add a pile of pegs, some dining chairs and a clothes airer (if not being used) into the room

* The kids now have all the equipment they need for a perfect fake fort minus the foraging for muddy sticks among stinging nettles

* This activity can go on for hours, and can take up lots of space depending on how well the sheets and blankets stay put and the imaginations run wild. It can provide a fun sleepover area too if you throw a duvet and snuggly pillow into the mix

98. Home-made lava lamp hack

A lava lamp was a thing of amazement when I was young, and my children get the same cool wonder when they watch one too. But did you know you can make one easily and cheaply, and get the added satisfaction of doing a bit of science-y stuff too?

★ Take an empty bottle (we use an empty water bottle or fizzy bottle) and fill it about three-quarters of the way with any cooking oil of your choice – I use sunflower oil

★ Fill a separate jug half full with water and stir in a couple of drops of food colouring of your choice

★ Pour your coloured water into the oil bottle and watch the oil and water separate, with the oil staying its original colour

★ Now pop in an effervescent tablet – one is normally enough, but you can add two if you like – and watch the coloured bubbly water move up and down in the oil!

★ Your kids will be entertained for ages watching this and can make their own versions with different food colours

99. Non-sticky slime hack

If your kids love slime like mine (poetry is also my thing!), but you're not so keen on the stickiness of the mix (and, let's face it, slime does seem to get everywhere), this will be right up your street.

And the best thing is you don't need to fork out on any expensive sticky slime mix kit either – you should have everything you need at home.

- Fill a cup half full of shaving foam
- Fill the rest of the cup with PVA glue and mix it together
- If you find the mixture is still a bit sticky, add a tiny bit of water to the mix
- If you want your slime any other colour, pop on a pair of gloves and mix in a couple of drops of food colouring
- Once it's all mixed you have your very own non-sticky super slime

100. Modelling clay for fine motor skills hack

Working on your child's fine motor skills helps develop their strength and coordination, which encourages them to become more independent when it comes to smaller movements like buttoning up coats and holding a pen.

This fun little hack will not only keep them focused for a while but will help with these important small muscle tasks.

* Take some modelling clay and squish it into a mound shape on the table

* Push some uncooked spaghetti into the clay so it looks a little bit like a long-spiked hedgehog

* Pop a small bowl of O-shaped breakfast cereal next to your 'hedgehog' and invite your kids to 'thread' the Os onto the spaghetti sticks

MAJOR MUM
HACKS VIDEO

101. Glow-in-the-dark bowling hack

Bowling is a lot of fun but it can be super expensive to go to the lanes as a family once you factor in a couple of games, drinks, etc.

So bowling at home – in the dark – is likely to make you the top scorer in the family as you challenge everyone to get strikes with the lights off!

★ Take as many empty plastic bottles as you can – I find small water bottles are best for this – and place an activated glow stick into each bottle

★ At one end of the room, place the bottles in a triangle shape so that you have one bottle at the front and then the others coming out behind at the sides. Then put all the soft balls you want to roll at the other end of the room ready for the bowlers.

★ Now turn off the lights and invite your family into the room for a bowling-in-the-dark experience – no hire shoes required!

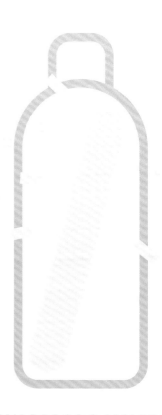

102. Icing hack for biscuit decorating

Biscuit decorating is one of my all-time favourite activities that involves little cost, lots of enjoyment and plenty of creative imagination – the possibilities and themes are endless.

This is a basic hack for biscuit decorating that can be built upon for different occasions, and gives you a starting point for some more fancy ideas.

⭐ Take a packet of your favourite plain biscuits (we love plain digestives) and set them out on little plates for each child

⭐ Using a plastic make-up organiser, put different coloured icing tubes in each compartment so the children can easily help themselves to their favourite colours

⭐ If smaller children find it tricky to squeeze out the icing, put the tubes in a cup of boiling water for a minute or two and then back into the organiser. The water will soften the icing and make it easier to pipe out

MAJOR MUM
HACKS VIDEO

103. Muffin tray hack

You know how much muffin trays come to the rescue in lots of these hacks, but here's another example of their use – a little snacktivity!

This hack will hopefully allow for a bit of housework to be done while the kids are entertained. Or maybe you can enjoy a cup of coffee … while it's still hot!

* Fill a muffin tray with one item in each compartment. Think little picky bits like fruit cereal, cut-up grapes/strawberries/cucumber, mini marshmallows, etc.

* Once you have filled it – this doesn't have to be to the top – take some magnetic tiles and cover each compartment

* Kids can then choose which compartment to try first before sampling another, and once they have eaten all their snacks they can play with the magnetic tiles afterwards – which should give you time for a second brew!

104. Colour disappearing hack

This is a brilliant and mind-blowing science hack that will have little and big kids alike gawping in amazement as the experiment unfolds. Trust me, you'll be wishing you paid more attention to your science teacher back in the day!

- ⭐ Draw a simple picture – I find a rainbow works well as it's very colourful

- ⭐ Put the picture in a plastic sandwich bag and seal it

- ⭐ With a black permanent marker, go over the outline of the drawing directly on top of the bag

- ⭐ Now take a glass bowl, fill it with water and lower the bag into it

- ⭐ Prepare to be amazed as the picture inside disappears! Let me explain further …

- ⭐ Refraction happens when light changes direction or bends when it moves from one material to another, so light travelling through air changes direction when it hits the water

- ⭐ And it's this that makes it look like the colours magically disappear!

Special occasions can be times when you feel you need to be on your A-game but, for one reason or another, fill you with more fear than a toddler on a play date suddenly going quiet … Panic!

The hacks in this section cover a range of celebratory occasions, from birthdays and Valentine's Day to Easter, Halloween and Christmas, but they can also be adapted for lots of other special events like Chinese New Year, Eid and Diwali depending on what traditions and celebrations are important to you and your family. Ultimately I want these hacks to help you overcome the most seemingly stressful situations because, if you too can enjoy the moments that matter, well, that's all that matters!

You've got this!

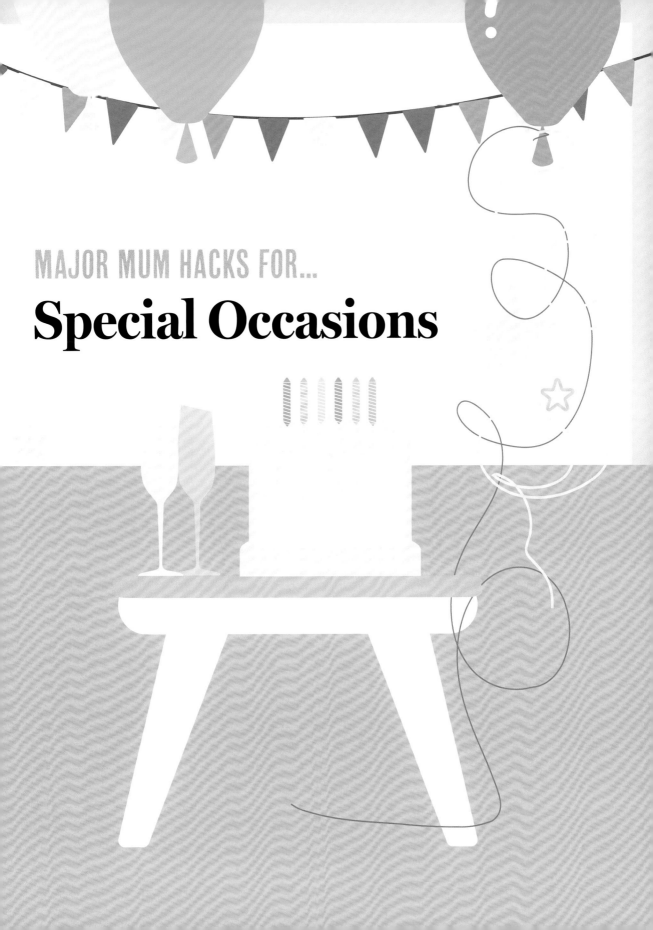

MAJOR MUM HACKS FOR...

Special Occasions

105. Cutting cake hack

Think dental floss is just to keep your pearly whites clean and your dentist impressed? Think again!

Birthday party venues don't always allow sharp knives due to various health and safety polices, which can be a bit tricky when you have birthday cake to share out into party bags. But, don't panic, a dental hygiene tool can help you overcome this!

- ★ Take with you to the party or venue a roll of unflavoured, unscented dental floss

- ★ Once everyone has sung happy birthday and you've taken all the photos you need, tell them it's time for the floss!

- ★ While the kids are moving and shaking and doing the classic dance move, you are expertly cutting through the cake having secured a suitable length of dental floss around fingers on both hands

- ★ Hold the floss firmly and bring it down over the cake all the way to the bottom, repeating as many times as necessary

- ★ Now let them eat cake!

106. Gift card pictures hack

Birthday parties for your children can be big, loud and raucous affairs, with a table piled high with pressies that your lucky birthday child can't wait to unwrap.

But all the chaos of excited unwrapping can sometimes mean you don't know who gave you what and who to thank.

 ⋆ Instead of trying to make a list as you go, take a quick photo of each present as it's unwrapped, with the card or label next to it

 ⋆ You then have a reference when you and your child come to write thank you notes, or for when you next see the person to thank them verbally

 ⋆ Alternatively, you could send a photo of your child with their unwrapped present to the person as a thank you snap instead – either as a photo card or as a phone message to save you time

107. Cake fresh hack

Cake solves pretty much every crisis you might encounter in life, so we never like to turn down a slice. But we also don't like the idea of a piece of cake drying out and not being as fantastically fresh as we'd like (reader, we still would munch).

With a self-made cake box, your slice will stay yummy for longer and you can transport your precious cargo home safely.

★ Take a piece of baking/parchment paper and put it on the side of the slice of cake, flipping the cake on to the paper so it sticks

★ Put the cake onto the lid of a plastic storage box, using it as a base

★ Then take the box itself and place it over the cake so you can transport it easily and the cake stays moist

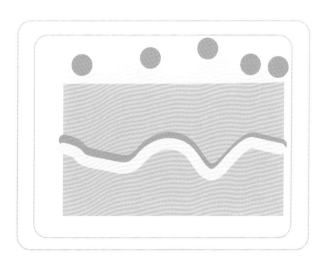

108. Helium balloons hack

Helium balloons do create an amazing 'wow' effect at birthday parties or events but they are blimmin' expensive – especially if you are trying to fill a large room. Which is why I love this really simple and cheap hack that uses normal balloons instead.

* Because non-helium balloons are a lot cheaper and come in so many styles and colours, buy in bulk as many as you want for your occasion and inflate as normal

* Add a glue dot to each one you want as your fake helium balloon and start sticking them to the ceiling

* Tie ribbons from the bottom for the full effect and create a ceiling full of beautiful balloons for less than half the price of helium ones

* Glue dots can also be used to stick the balloons together, so be creative with your ideas and have fun!

109. Character cupcakes hack

Cupcakes are a great idea for youngsters' birthday parties, but if your little one is in love with a particular TV or film character, or you are having a themed party, character cupcakes can cost you a small fortune. And, let's face it, cupcakes get half eaten or dropped anyway, which can make you see red if you've spent a lot.

★ Have a look online for edible character toppers for cakes and buy as many as you need

★ Head to the supermarket and buy some plain own-brand cupcakes

★ Make up some plain icing and put it on top, then stick your internet-bought character toppers on top

110. Heart-shaped cupcake hack

These will make your kids' hearts beat a little faster when it's baking time, as they are not only yummy to eat but super fun to make too. And the heart shapes just melt our, er, hearts. Plus, as pink is one of my favourite colours in the world, I don't need many excuses to make the cake mixture, icing and toppings all perfectly pink!

★ Make the cupcakes following your own cupcake recipe as normal, but make sure you add some pink food colouring too

★ Place the mixture into cupcake cases, filling them about halfway

★ Taking some tinfoil, roll some of it into little balls and fold some into smaller square parcel shapes

★ Put a foil ball at the top of each cupcake, between the case and the tin, to make the rounded top of the heart

★ Put the smaller square bits into each side, to give the case its heart shape

★ Cook the cupcakes in the oven as per your recipe instructions and then bring out to cool. The cake mixture will now have cooked to make the heart shape

★ Take a tub of shop-bought pink icing and whisk it up – this makes it a lot more creamy and fluffy – then add a layer to your cupcake hearts before finishing with some edible heart sprinkles on top

111. Napkin heart hack

I love setting the table for the kids when it's Valentines Day – it makes the whole day feel a little bit more lovely and puts everyone in a feel-good mood.

This is a simple hack that your kids will love to see and will spend ages trying to copy – and it makes V-Day brekkie a little more special, because who doesn't want a heart napkin with their cereal and toast?

⋆ Take a red paper napkin (of course, any paper napkin will do if you don't have red, but we like to get with the theme!)

⋆ Open it up so that you have the two squares and then fold upwards so that you have a long rectangle shape

⋆ Using your finger in the middle, bring up one side to your finger so it's pointing upwards and then do the same to the other side

⋆ Fold down the middle bit of each side and tuck it underneath

⋆ Now, to neaten the edges of the heart, fold down the outer edges of each side and fold underneath

⋆ We heart this hack so much

MAJOR MUM
HACKS VIDEO

112. Valentine's Day giant sweet hack

Making a giant sweet is a sure-fire way to win the heart of your partner – Mr Major Mum Hacks, take note – but you really don't have to wait until Valentine's Day to make these, you could adapt the sweets for birthdays, Christmas or just as fun end-of-term treats for the kids.

I love spoiling my lot with these big treats, the sweets inside are all individual favourites for them and they are so excited when they get one, they don't want to open them up!

* Take two paper bowls and fill one of them with love-related goodies – heart-shaped chocs, sweets, etc. – or any of their favourite treats or according to the theme of the occasion (e.g. pumpkin chocs for Halloween)

* Then use sticky tape to secure the other bowl on top, facing down like a lid

* Using a red paper tablecloth, cut down to size, pink tissue paper or heart-printed wrapping paper, put the bowl of sweets in the middle and then fold over and tape

* Now scrunch together the ends of the paper either side of the bowl and secure with some pretty ribbon. Your giant sweet treat is ready! Just don't tell your dentist

113. Cloud dough hack

For a sensory treat for little ones and an alternative to slime, cloud dough is easy to make and fun to play with. Give it a few drops of pink or red colouring and call it Valentine's dough. Your little ones will love playing with it for hours and you'll love cleaning up afterwards – not for hours!

★ Pour one cup of hair conditioner into a mixing bowl (find a cheap variety for this, you don't want to use your best)

★ Take two cups of cornstarch and add to the bowl

★ Add one or two drops of pink or red food dye and some Valentine's Day heart confetti

★ Mix it all together and then, when it's fully mixed, take it out and knead the dough with your hands until it's smooth

★ You now have a perfect slime alternative for little ones (or big ones) to play with

114. Ice cube chocolate strawberries hack

Nothing says love on Valentine's Day like strawberries and chocolate, which is rather silly really when you think that both these ingredients are readily available all year. I think the idea of doing something different with them is a nice treat for the special day and I love this easy way of creating a yummy pudding to finish off a romantic meal … or as a treat for myself after vacuuming the living room. Either occasion works!

☆ Melt some chocolate either in the microwave or over a pan of boiling water

☆ Pour the melted chocolate into a clean and empty ice-cube tray

☆ Put a strawberry on top of each cube section, pointy end down, and place in the freezer

☆ Take out after a couple of hours and carefully pop out the strawberries, which now have a nice coating of chocolate on top. Heaven!

115. Easter bunny cakes hack

This is such a simple yet effective way to make bunny shaped cupcakes, and a great activity to do with the kids in the Easter hols. They make cute little gifts for older family members too if you want to give them something a little more personal than a shop-bought egg.

★ Make cupcakes following your own cupcake recipe as normal

★ Start pouring the mixture into cupcake cases, but only fill up halfway

★ Take a small piece of tinfoil and roll into three separate small balls, put one at the top bit of the cake mix, between the case and the tin, and put the other two balls one on each side, between the case and the tin, to give a bunny face shape. Do this for each cupcake case.

★ Cook the cupcakes in the oven as per your recipe instructions and then bring out to cool. The cake mixture will now have cooked to make the bunny shape

★ Ice your cupcakes with white or grey rolled icing, slightly scoring the icing so it looks like fur, and then diagonally cut a mini marshmallow and put where the ear shapes have been created. Be warned, this will probably look too cute to eat!

MAJOR MUM
HACKS VIDEO

116. Glow-in-the-dark egg hunt hack

We love using glow sticks in our house and you'll find them used in lots of the hacks in this book, for which I make no apology. This is a cool glow-in-the-dark spin on your regular egg hunt, plus if the good old British weather isn't playing ball and you can't hide your eggs outside, just turn off all the lights inside and let your kids get hunting!

⭐ Buy a packet of glow sticks and a number of clear plastic eggs (you'll find these quite cheaply on craft websites and in craft shops)

⭐ Activate the glow sticks and put one inside each egg to hide around your house. Or, if the rain has stopped, you could do this in your garden at night-time

⭐ Tell the kids to bring their baskets, turn off all the lights or wait for it to get dark, and find those eggs!

HACK THE HACK:

If you like being super creative, you could also buy some cheap glow-in-the dark paint and paint the eggs to hide around the house. Or do this as a daytime activity with the kids, leave the eggs to dry and, once hidden, they will have the excitement of trying to find their own special egg.

MAJOR MUM HACKS VIDEO

117. Toy building blocks Easter egg hack

If you want to do something different this Easter to reduce the amount of chocolate your kids are gorging on, this is a fun alternative to hunting chocolate eggs.

And as this is more of an activity-type egg hunt, you'll find it provides more entertainment for the kids than just finding and eating chocolate. And if your children like to build brick models, but once they have made something it's left untouched, this is a cool way to reuse toys they already have.

★ If you don't want to buy a small box of building blocks specifically for this task, break up an old creation and fish out the instruction booklet (I keep these for this very reason)

★ Take some plastic eggs and fill them with one or two building blocks each until the whole creation has been distributed into eggs. You won't want to choose the Millennium Falcon for this – aim for something a lot smaller!

★ Once your kids have found all the eggs you can give them a clue to where the instruction booklet is, so they can then try to make their product. If they aren't too keen on building blocks, you could hide little nail varnishes, stickers or small puzzles instead

118. Balloon egg hunt hack

There is nothing I enjoy more than hiding lots of little eggs around the garden for my kids to find – the squeals of delight when they find them are unmatched. But there have been occasions when I've forgotten where I have hidden all the eggs, which causes all sorts of problems when one kid has found more than the other and I know I have counted out an equal amount.

This hack not only helps me remember where all the eggs I've hidden are, it also gives toddlers a big clue as to where to look. Plus, if you have invited friends round to egg hunt with your kids, they can take home a balloon as an extra treat!

* ★ Buy some cheap helium balloons (you don't need fancy ones, but there is usually a fun collection of Easter-themed ones around if you are tempted) and line up an egg with a balloon so you know you have enough of each

* ★ Cut some lengths of string or ribbon and tie a piece around the end of each helium balloon, then carefully secure the other end of the string or ribbon around each egg you want to hide. You could use masking tape for this if you can't make a strong enough knot

* ★ I like to cut the string or ribbon into different lengths so the balloons fill more space and are easy to spot – and visually I think this looks more fun too

119. Sheep cupcake hack

Chicks, bunnies and lambs doth an Easter make, so if you want to make sure you've got the sheep-related part of that covered, why not try to make some baa-utiful sheep cupcakes as a fun Easter activity. Like the bunny cakes (Hack 115), these make great little gifts too.

⭑ Buy some cheap, plain cupcakes and make a bowl of buttercream icing

⭑ Take the cupcakes out of their paper cases and spoon a small amount of icing onto each cupcake, then start covering each one with mini marshmallows until you have a fluffy sheep body

⭑ Add in some edible eyes with some edible glue – both are cheap and can be bought from most supermarkets or online

⭑ Carefully cut a small chocolate egg in half and add it to the front of your cupcake using the edible glue

⭑ Carefully break a crispy-candy covered chocolate in half to create two ears and add to the top of the cupcake using the edible glue

⭑ Continue until you have completed all your cupcakes in the same way

⭑ Pop the cakes in the fridge for 10 minutes

⭑ After that, your sheep will be ready to be rounded up and, er, eaten!

120. Lemonade pancakes hack

We love Pancake Day in our house, which means I like to experiment with different mixtures and ingredients so we always end up getting the best flippin' pancakes in town.

- ★ Take a mixing bowl and pour in the pancake mixture

- ★ Instead of adding the amount of milk specified in the instructions, use lemonade instead – maybe just a smidgeon less than stated

- ★ Mix up the lemonade and pancake mixture with a whisk and then spoon onto a hot frying pan

- ★ The lemonade makes the pancakes sweet tasting and light, and if you want to add a couple of white chocolate buttons too (because why wouldn't you?) pop them on top and then a little bit more mixture on top of that before you flip the first time

- ★ Cook on both sides and then serve with some syrup

HACK THE HACK:
If you want to make your pancakes a cool zigzag shape then mix the batter as you normally would and put it into an empty ketchup container. You'll be able to squirt out any shape you want – plus you can control your standard round pancake shape too. And pizza cutters are simply the best utensil when it comes to cutting pancakes, much easier than using a knife!

121. Pancake tray bake hack

Sometimes making pancakes can take a while, not in terms of prep but because each person wants their own, so you are left in front of the pan adding mixture, flipping and serving for each child.

This tray bake hack cuts that time right out, leaving you more time for eating pancakes, plus you'll be able to keep them for longer so Pancake Day can be Pancake Three Days!

* Take a baking tray and line it with baking paper

* Pour on your pancake mix and then add your choice of toppings. Each person can have their own section of pancake mix, which means you can add as many toppings as you like and it's all done in one cook

* Bake in the oven at 175°C (345°F) until lightly golden

* The pancake is now ready to eat, or you can keep it for up to three days in an airtight container

122. American pancakes hack

Experimenting with ingredients to add to a pancake is always fun, but one of the faves in our house is the American-style pancake where I add some bacon into the mix – it's like we are in a diner in the US of A every time we sit and eat it!

★ Place some strips of bacon in the oven and cook until crispy

★ Remove from the oven and leave to cool so you can cut them into smaller chunks

★ Pour some pancake mix onto the grill pan and then add a sprinkling of the bacon, finishing with another dribble of pancake mix on top of that

★ Flip when ready and serve with a dollop of syrup. And have a nice day y'all!

123. Copycat coffee shop twists hack

These chocolate custard twists are one of my favourite copycat recipes to make with the kids. This not only saves a ton of money (sorry high-street coffee shops!) but they are fun to make too.

Ingredients-wise you'll only need two boxes of puff pastry, a tin or pot of ready-made custard, some chocolate chips and a bit of milk to brush over before baking, and although these might not technically be pancakes, they are a flipping good alternative.

- ★ Roll out one sheet of puff pastry onto some baking paper and then spread over an even layer of custard (you'll probably only need a couple of dollops of this for spreading, so you can keep the rest of the custard for another occasion)

- ★ Sprinkle over the chocolate chips so they are evenly distributed and then add the other sheet of puff pastry on top

- ★ Using a pizza cutter, cut into six strips and then twist each strip over once in the middle (you can do more if you prefer thinner strips)

- ★ Brush some milk over the top then cook in the oven for 20–25 minutes at 200ºC (390ºF) before taking out to cool and then tucking into this choccie-custard twisted delight

MAJOR MUM
HACKS VIDEO

124. Pumpkin drink holder hack

This is such a fun way to serve drinks at a Halloween party, but if you are not liking the idea of cleaning out a pumpkin or are worried it's going to be super messy, don't panic (see 'Hack the Hack').

★ Buy an XL pumpkin and cut a hole at the bottom – you want the top of the pumpkin intact

★ Remove all the insides as per my instructions in 'Hack the Hack', and then cut a small hole in the front of the pumpkin – this is for your drink's tap dispenser, so cut the size accordingly

★ Take a drinks bag – you can find these easily online – and put it inside the pumpkin, checking everything fits and the tap bit sits through the smaller hole you made

★ Fill your drinks bag with either kids' fruit squash or an adult beverage, and your new drinks dispenser is ready to rumble!

HACK THE HACK:
Removing the inside of a pumpkin doesn't need to be messy and long-winded. Start by using a scoop to get the bigger bits out of the way, then use an electric whisk to remove the rest. Your pumpkin will be hollowed out in no time!

125. Pumpkin flower vase hack

If you thought pumpkins were just for carving, think again! This is a great centrepiece to have on your table or you can make lovely seasonal vases to have dotted around the house in the run-up to Halloween.

* Cut a hole in the top of your pumpkin and scrape out all the insides using a scoop and then an electric whisk (see Hack 124 for more info on this)

* Once it's cleaned out, wash the inside with a bit of water and bleach to stop it going mouldy (see 'Hack the Hack')

* Take an empty and clean tin can and pop inside the pumpkin through the top hole

* Add some water to the tin can and then place some autumnal flowers in the top

HACK THE HACK:

If you have loads of pumpkins that you are planning on carving or having around your house, once you have cleaned them out pop them all in the bath – or a bucket if you only have a couple – and fill with cold water until they are submerged. Then add a couple of squirts of bleach to the water and leave them for about 10 minutes before taking them out and drying them off. This will help keep them fresh, stop bacteria growing on them and they should last up to four weeks.

126. Ring doughnut spiders hack

My kids go crazy for this, which is hilarious as they aren't such big fans of normal spiders ... apparently doughnut ones are a different matter!

★ Buy a packet of plain ring doughnuts – glazed ones are great, but avoid colourful ones that are iced

★ Take a packet of small black sandwich cookies and place a biscuit into the middle of each doughnut

★ Using some edible glue, stick some edible eyes on to each biscuit and then, with some black tube icing, squirt out lines either side of the biscuit, over the side of the doughnut, to make the spider's legs

★ I guarantee your kids won't be running away when you bring out a plate of these spiders ...

127. Surgical gloves party favours hack

A Halloween party requires Halloween favours and so, to make it super spooky, why not use surgical gloves instead of party bags?

You can get a big box of these online (these gloves come in handy for all sorts of things – see Hack 128, for example) and if you have a lot of kids at your party, these really are a cheap way of handing out favours.

* Buy some longer sweets for the fingers – marshmallows twists pushed down make the fingers stand out and look really lifelike

* Then fill the rest with some other sweets of your choice and put in some plastic creepy crawlies too, in keeping with the theme

* Tie up each 'hand' like you would a balloon, or use ribbon instead. You can write names on them if you are giving them to specific children or place all the hands in a large box for them to help themselves

128. Frozen hand and worm ice cube hack

A combination of our two favourite frozen hacks that is perfect for thrills and squeals of delight at a Halloween party.

* ★ Take a surgical glove and fill it with water, then tie the end securely before popping it in the freezer

* ★ Take a packet of jelly worms and wind them into ice cube trays, one per square – you might need to cut them in two depending on the length of your worms

* ★ Fill the tray up with water over the sweets and pop it in the freezer too

* ★ When it's nearly time for your guests to arrive, take the hand out of the freezer and remove the glove before placing the hand into your prepared drinks bowl and you have a creepy frozen Halloween hand punch

* ★ The iced worms can be left in the freezer until the kids start asking for a drink, then you can add them to their cups and listen out for the screams – of delight!

129. Spider hair/ghost hair hack

I can't tell you how flipping fun this is to do and how effective it is – forget a boring old witch's hat, your kid's head will be their crowning glory at the Halloween party thanks to these two boo-tiful barnet ideas.

For spider hair:

★ Put your kid's hair into a bun in the middle of their head

★ Cover it with a black napkin and secure it with a black hair tie so it looks like a black blob

★ Take some black pipe cleaners and twist them around the bun so that the ends come out as legs

★ Using self-adhesive googly eyes, stick them onto the blob body and, hey presto, you have spider-bun hair!

For ghostly hair:

★ Put your kid's hair into two buns, one on each side of their head

★ Take four or five squares of toilet paper and lay them on top of each other at different angles so they aren't all square

★ Place them over one bun and secure with a white hair band, then repeat on the other side

★ Using a black pen, draw two eyes on each ghost and get ready to say boo!

MAJOR MUM
HACKS VIDEO

130. Slow cooker hack

If you've invited friends over to your house for a night of fireworks and sparklers, this is the perfect way to provide quick and easy food without spending hours on preparation or worrying about cooking on the night. No one wants to be slaving away in the kitchen when the Catherine wheel gets going!

⭐ Cook some sausages and put them into hot dog buns before covering each one with some tinfoil

⭐ Put your slow cooker on a low heat for about an hour before your guests arrive and put all your wrapped hotdogs inside

⭐ Set up a little area for sauces, napkins, onions, etc., and let your guests help themselves to a yummy hotdog whenever they fancy

HACK THE HACK:
This slow cooker hack is great for jacket potatoes too. Simply cook up a batch and cover with tinfoil. Pop them in the slow cooker on a low heat and set up a filling station (cheese, coleslaw, etc.) next to it so your guests can help themselves when they fancy a bite to eat – and you are free to enjoy your evening too.

131. Ice cream cone s'mores hack

There is something special about a s'mores in wintertime, but melting marshmallows over a fire is a bit tricky for youngsters and can be messy and stressful all in one go, which takes the fun out of this yummy treat. And this is why ice cream cones can be your new best friends.

⭐ Take a packet of ice cream cones and fill them three-quarters of the way with marshmallows – mini ones are good, but you can use normal size ones too

⭐ Break some squares of chocolate on top or use chocolate buttons, and wrap each cone with tinfoil

⭐ If you have a fire pit with a grill, pop them on top of that or, alternatively, put the oven on and warm for about 15 minutes

⭐ Take them out of the oven or off the heat and let the kids enjoy a yummy firework night treat. Don't worry, you will have made some extra for the big kids too!

132. Toffee apple hack

Toffee apples and Bonfire Night go hand in hand, but all too often, while kids like the idea of them, the crunchy outer layer is hard to tackle and the majority of it goes to waste. Not so with this hack: yummy, sticky and edible!

★ Cut each apple into four segments using a cutter to take the core out

★ Add in a lolly stick – you can buy these really cheaply in bulk or keep old sticks from previously eaten lollies

★ Unwrap a packet of hard toffees and melt in the microwave for 1–2 minutes

★ Drip the melted toffee over the apples and decorate with some sprinkles for an added treat

★ For an alternative to toffees, use chocolate eclair sweets for some added chocolate on your apples too

133. Christmas gift bag hack

This is one of those hacks that I have people saying to me, 'I can't believe I didn't know this before!', and I was the same when I found out too. This is such an easy and effective way to make sure your Christmas gift bags are securely fastened and the presents inside all snug as a bug in a rug.

★ When you have wrapped your present (although the great thing about gift-bagging an item is that you can get away with putting some tissue paper on top of it) make sure it's at the bottom of the bag

★ Starting on one side, take the toggle at one end of the string and feed it through the hole on the opposite side, then do the same with the toggle on the other end

★ Repeat with the toggles on the other side, so that your toggle ends are now all securely pushed through the opposite sides

★ Finally, pull gently on the handles you have created and your bag comes together completely, no need to tape it across or leave it gaping open, your present is secure inside!

MAJOR MUM
HACKS VIDEO

134. Wrapping paper bag hack

This hack is a clever way of giving a gift without making a song or dance over getting it tightly wrapped – you'll be making your own gift bag for it instead.

Luckily for you I have a few of these ideas up my sleeve to make the seemingly never-ending task of wrapping presents less stressful and more enjoyable – and no gin or tonic required!

* I call this my teddy bear wrapping bag because, let's face it, soft toys are tricky to wrap and the end result can sometimes look like something your toddler hashed together – a mess!

* Start by measuring the width of the bear you have, don't worry about the height as you will be using the full length of wrapping roll

* Once you have the width measured – and make sure you then add a least another 5 cm either side – cut the paper and fold over the edges so they are neat

* Tape together the folded edges so that you have a 'tunnel' of paper and then take one end and fold into an envelope shape. This is the bottom of your bag so make sure you tape it up well once you have secured it

* Pop your teddy or soft toy inside and then fold down from the other end a couple of neat folds (approximately 2 cm each fold)

* When you have made a couple of folds, place some ribbon on top, making sure that you have left some long bits of ribbon either side as you will be using that to tie a bow at the end. Keep folding down some more so the ribbon is secure

* When you are near the top of the bear, stop rolling and simply fold the top over one last time, securing with tape, then take the two ends of the ribbon and bring together into a bow

135. Christmas socks wrapping hack

Teacher gifts can sometimes be a tricky one to get right, but more times than not we've found that a bottle of wine is usually a thoughtful and beneficial pressie for the hard-working teacher – and certainly beats an apple!

Bottle bags however can be boring and plain, so make things a little more personal and fun by wrapping the bottle in a pair of festive fluffy socks.

- ★ You can sometimes get some good deals on festive socks (three for two or buy one get one free) so if you have several gifts to give – dance teachers, football coaches, teaching assistants, they'll also love this treat – keep an eye out for sock deals

- ★ Place the bottle in one of the socks and then pull the sock up from the bottom

- ★ Take the other sock and wrap it round so that it forms a sort of bow or scarf around the bottle

- ★ The recipient of this gift (this is also a great idea for Secret Santa work colleague gifts) will have two pressies in one: a lovely tipple and a useful pair of festive socks

136. Wrapping paper cut too small hack

When you are wrapping what seems like a gazillion presents at Christmas time you can sometimes misjudge your paper cutting and present ratio. Which then leaves you with wasted paper and presents that still need wrapping.

Luckily for you, I'm like the wrapping fairy-hackmother and I'm here to help.

* If you have just cut the wrapping paper and found it doesn't quite stretch over the gift however many times you try (surely the fifth time of trying to stretch it over it will magically fit?) then twist it on the diagonal

* You need to have (if you are wrapping a box) the long sides of the present facing opposite corners of the wrapping paper

* Bring these corners into the centre, followed by the other two corners, and tape down

* Now everything fits snuggly underneath, no present on show and no need for extra paper. It's a small yet vital win at this time of year

MAJOR MUM
HACKS VIDEO

137. Christmas tree cheeseboard hack

This isn't a hack per se but a fabulously festive way of displaying your cheese for any Christmassy gathering you might have in the run-up to the big day.

You don't need an excuse for whipping out a cheeseboard of course, but this makes your Cheddar seem all the cheerier and your Stilton all the more satisfying.

★ Take out your chopping board or the board you are going to prepare your Christmas tree cheeseboard on

★ Start cutting the different cheeses into squares and put to one side

★ There is no set way of doing this but the idea is to display your nibbles in a Christmas tree shape, so I always start with something like salami slices at the bottom, followed by a section of cut-up cheese and then grapes, olives, more cheese, tomatoes (or whatever you like to use), but make sure as you go up that you make the different sections smaller and smaller

★ If you are feeling super fancy, cut a piece of Cheddar into a star shape and put it on the top of your tree

138. Rudolph strawberries hack

These are one of my favourite Christmassy things to make, partly because they are so easy yet so effective, and partly because Christmas to me is all about the magic of Santa and his reindeer, so creating Rudolph in food form is what it's all about!

I call this my Rudolph hack, but of course you can call it Dancer, Prancer, Donner or Blitzen … just remember to use a brown crispy-candy covered chocolate instead of a red one at the end!

* Boil a pan of water and place a bag of small chocolates in it

* While you leave the bag in for 5 minutes, cut off the leaf end of a strawberry so that it sits flat on a plate, then cut the top off too

* Remove the melted chocolate from the pan and dip your strawberries in it before putting them on a plate or tray covered in baking paper

* Pop in the fridge for 2–5 minutes and then remove

* Take some pretzels and stick them in the top for antlers and then put edible eyes on each one

* Finish off each one with a red crispy-candy covered chocolate for a nose and your Rudolphs are ready go!

MAJOR MUM
HACKS VIDEO

139. Grinch skewer hack

Christmas wouldn't be Christmas without the mean Mr Grinch making an appearance – albeit in grape and marshmallow form – but if your kids are fans of the green monster, they will love making this Whoville villain with you.

This is similar to the previous hack in that it's super effective on a party platter but takes next to no time to make.

- ★ Add a green grape to a cocktail stick and push down nearly all the way
- ★ Cut a slice of banana and push down next before adding an upside-down strawberry after that
- ★ Finally pop a mini marshmallow on top
- ★ Now you have the Grinch with his Santa hat, ready to gobble up

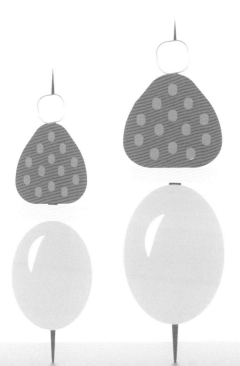

140. Melted snowman biscuit hack

Is there anything sadder than a melted snowman on the front lawn and a small pile of sticks, stones and a scarf on top where the little guy once stood?

Celebrate the melted snowman in all his glory by making a pretend-snow biscuit that combines all the fun of biscuit decorating with a twist.

★ Take a plain biscuit – either a digestive or rich tea – and drip on a layer of white icing so it looks like it's melted onto the top, not perfectly covered

★ Take a medium-sized white marshmallow and stick it on towards one edge of the biscuit, decorating one side using black icing for eyes and mouth

★ If you have some orange icing, put a carrot nose on the marshmallow and then take some mini crispy-candy covered chocolates and add them to the biscuit too, as buttons

★ Use the black icing again to pipe some stick hands on to the biscuit and you now have yourself a sad little melted snow-friend – albeit a yummy one

141. Christmas pudding crispy rice hack

Crispy cakes aren't just for Easter, when you make a little nest for your mini eggs to sit in – the basis of those yummy delights can be made into mini Chrimbo puds too.

And we know we're probably in the minority here, but much better than the real thing in our opinion – even with brandy butter!

★ Take a mixing bowl and add in 200 g of crispy rice and 6 tbsp of golden syrup

★ In a separate pan or bowl, melt 100 g of butter, add to your mixing bowl then melt 200 g of milk chocolate and add that to the bowl too, then mix all the ingredients together

★ Roll your mixture into ball shapes, place them onto baking paper and pop in the fridge for about an hour

★ When the hour is nearly up, melt 100 g of white chocolate so it's ready for when you remove your puds, then dribble it on top, aiming for about a third of each pud to be covered

★ Using some green icing, add some holly leaves and roll some red icing into little balls to make the berries. Yummy!

142. Christmas slow cooker hot chocolate hack

Hot chocolate and a Christmas film is what winter weekend afternoons are made for, but if your kids have got their friends round for a cinema afternoon, you might as well get used to being in the kitchen, the amount of time you'll be spending by the kettle making mugs of yummy hot choc.

This slow cooker hack will eliminate all that time faffing around, which means you can join in the movie fun too.

- ⭐ Take your slow cooker and pour in 1 litre of whole milk and 300 ml of double cream

- ⭐ Break 100 g of plain milk chocolate into small pieces and add to the pot, giving it a good stir

- ⭐ Put the lid on the slow cooker and leave on a low heat setting for a couple of hours, stirring after about an hour

- ⭐ Take the lid off and cook for another 30 minutes while you line up the mugs and marshmallows

- ⭐ Then invite all your guests to come to you while you ladle chocolate heaven into their cups and sprinkle with a few mini marshmallows on top

- ⭐ If you want to make an adult version of this, add 150 ml of Baileys into the mix at the beginning

143. Salt paint hack

This is a lovely little craft idea if you want to make an alternative Christmas card for grandparents or maybe as a teacher's end of term gift. It's a different way of painting because it doesn't require any, er, paint. Which also means it doesn't make as much mess – it's like the most perfect painting hack ever!

★ Take some dark-coloured paper – black or navy is great or, because it's Christmas, dark red will work brilliantly too

★ Dissolve a cup full of salt in boiling water and wait for it to cool. Your kids might enjoy seeing all the salt magically disappear as you stir, and you can take turns guessing how long it will take

★ Now give the kids a clean/dry paintbrush and get them to paint snowflake or snowman patterns or shapes on the paper, or names if you have a thin enough brush

★ Let the salt water dry and you will have some cool wintery crystal paintings on your paper

144. New Year's tree hack

If you get sad taking down all your Christmas tree decorations but equally don't want to be the person that has a houseful of tinsel mid-May, this hack helps you get the most out of your Norwegian pine by giving it its own New Year celebration.

★ On New Year's Eve – or before, depending on when you put away your decorations – take all the Christmas decs off your tree so you are left with a blank canvas

★ You might already have a collection of New Year's ornaments (some shops have started selling these) or you might want to decorate with your own New Year decorations: you could take a separate packet of plain baubles and write on them the year you are soon to be welcoming in with marker pen, or get the family to write down their resolutions or what they are excited about in the coming year

★ If you are having a New Year's Eve party, you could invite your guests to decorate a bauble with their own wishes for the upcoming year or add their own personal decoration

HACK THE HACK:
If you are going to keep your tree up longer than usual but are fed up with all the pine needles dropping, use a lint roller to pick them up for you. These clothes de-fluffers are brilliant for picking up pine needles for a quick and easy clear-up.

145. Cold bubbly hack

Toasting the New Year with a glass of bubbly is a must in our house, but there have been occasions amid all the excitement of the countdown that I have forgotten to pop the champers in the fridge to cool.

If you find yourself like me at 11.30 pm and need a quick way of cooling down your bottle of fizz before midnight, this cool hack is for you.

- ★ Wet a piece of kitchen roll with cold water and wrap it around the bottle so it covers it

- ★ Put it in the freezer for 15–20 minutes

- ★ As the countdown ends, you'll find you have a chilled bottle of bubbles ready to be poured in celebration. Happy New Year!

146. Balloon countdown for children hack

This is a great way to help your children be part of the countdown, especially younger children who need a bit of help telling the time but want to know how long they have got to go until the clock strikes midnight.

Blow up a number of balloons to represent the hours leading up to midnight. I start from 3 pm so I have ten balloons, but you can go as early or as late as you like, just adjust your number of balloons accordingly.

★ Once you have blown up your balloons, write the hour on each one – 3 pm, 4 pm, 5 pm, etc. – and line them up on a shelf or kitchen worktop

★ Each hour, the kids can pop the relevant balloon number, which also acts as a visual guide to see how much longer they have to go

★ Alternatively, you could hide balloons around the house and get your kids to hunt the relevant number balloon when you call out the time. You'll feel a bit like Big Ben by midnight!

147. Countdown party bags hack

I love doing party goodie bags and filling them with bits for the kids, and this is a similar idea crossed with a super-quick advent calendar. The idea is to keep the kids entertained throughout the evening while giving them something exciting to look forward to each hour.

Decide on when you want your countdown to begin and plan your party bag fillers accordingly. As with the previous hack, I tend to opt for starting around 3 pm, giving me ten gift bags to make, but you can make as many or as few as you like.

★ Don't think these hourly gift boxes or goodie bags need to be filled with extravagant pressies, especially if you are doing them for lots of children. I use little cupcake boxes for each hour and put a sweet, a few colouring pens or a small fidget toy in each one

★ You could line them up on the table for the kids to collect each hour, or bring them out each time another hour passes. If you have older children, they could be in charge of dishing them out as the clock ticks down

148. DIY balloon drop hack

There is something super cool about watching balloons cascade down onto an audience when you see it on TV at big concerts or events, but they are so easy to make for your own New Year's Eve party that I've been using them for years. And they are a focal point of excitement when the clock strikes midnight!

★ Get hold of a plastic or paper tablecloth (you might already have one or you can buy them cheaply online or at the supermarket), or use a sheet

★ Secure it to the ceiling using masking tape at each of the four corners, making sure it's not pulled tightly otherwise you won't have any space between the tablecloth or sheet and the ceiling to add in your balloons

★ Start blowing up and adding as many balloons as you want – colours and designs completely up to you

★ When midnight strikes, gather the children underneath and, using a friend and a chair each, stand at opposite corners and unstick the tape, releasing the balloons onto the excitable screams below

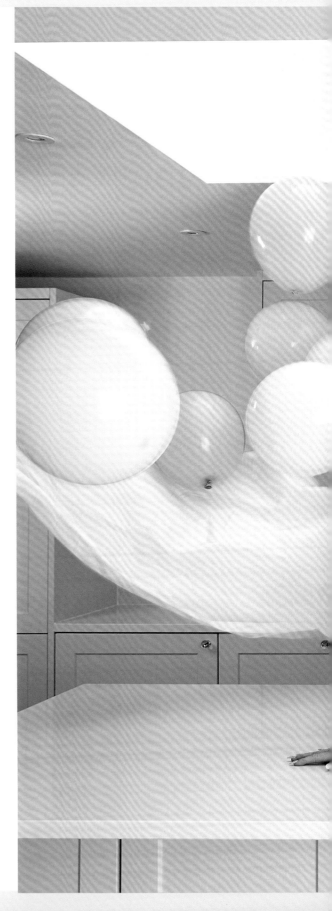

149. Candyfloss mocktail hack

Older children might not get that excited about party bags or countdown balloons, so make sure they don't miss out on some of the excitement of NYE with their own special fake-Prosecco mocktail to toast the New Year.

★ Take a plastic champagne flute and add some candy floss into the bottom

★ Then fill the rest of the glass with lemonade

★ Not only will it look like pink Prosecco, so they will feel like they are having a glass of champers like you, it will taste super sweet and give them something extra to have as a more grown-up treat

★ You could also set up a mocktail station and menu for pre-teens to create their own concoctions and try their hand at mixology

150. Early midnight countdown hack

Staying up until midnight is a big ask for little ones but trying to get them off to bed before midnight is equally hard if they have their hearts set on staying up to see in the New Year. Nothing is more stubborn than a child who is told it's bedtime when they are adamant they are not tired.

This might be a slightly misleading hack for children, but at the end of the year it's a win-win for everyone.

★ If your children are savvy when it comes to telling the time, this hack might take a little more prep, but it's still very doable – you'll just have to change all the clocks they look at around the house, and their nightlight if they have one that tells the time

★ Go onto YouTube about half an hour before you want to create your 'fake' midnight and look up a video of a previous London New Year's Eve countdown – you'll find lots of them online so you'll be spoilt for choice

★ When it's bedtime, simply pop the YouTube countdown on the telly and go through all the motions of seeing in the New Year. Your kids will be so excited they stayed up so late and celebrated with you they'll be full of tired excitement and ready for bed

★ And as it's only 7.37 pm, you'll be able to enjoy either a restful evening or give it a few hours then up the wooden hill to Bedfordshire yourself – midnight is late whatever age you are!

One last thing …

If you have reached the end of my book – well done! I always say that on my Instagram hacks don't I?! Well, the same applies here. There is one more thing I want to share with you – it's my last and best hack I have for being a mum and one that will change your life and your kids' lives for ever – and that is, don't be afraid to say 'sorry' or 'I was wrong.'

Being a mum is the best, yet most challenging job in the world. We get paid in the currency of love and pride as our children grow, but sometimes we mess things up. And that's OK. There will be times that every mum will lose her crap at least once (let's be realistic, it's probably more double figures). Kids push our buttons and, on those days, when we feel overwhelmed, it's OK to sit down and tell your kids 'I'm sorry, I'm not on my A-game today', or 'Sorry, I'm struggling today.' No one is perfect – we all make mistakes.

Your child will see you apologising, which will be a huge lesson for them in accepting responsibility themselves in life. It's a major life hack.

And, finally, please, please, never forget you are someone's whole world, and you are amazing.

Lots of love,

Casey x
aka Major Mum Hacks

Notes!